BRIDGING
THE GAP

BRIDGING THE GAP

*Youth and Adults
in the Church*

Merton P. Strommen

AUGSBURG PUBLISHING HOUSE
MINNEAPOLIS, MINNESOTA

A special thank you to my wife, Irene, to my assistant, Shelby Andress, and the two who typed my manuscript: Solveig Heintz and Katherine Rouzer.

BRIDGING THE GAP

Manufactured in the United States of America

Contents

Preface

Youth of ages 15-23, the focus in this book, are a historic group. The eyes of the nation were upon them as they joined the extraordinary baby boom of the years 1948-1953. During this short period there was a 50% increase in births. By 1965 the center of population gravity was the youngest in our history since the early nineteenth century.

In 1970, when the data were collected for A Study of Generations, a large-scale research study of Lutherans, a decade of profound change among young people came to an end. Youth in our studies reflect this change. In 1959, few were concerned over national and world issues. By 1970 they were the most concerned group, outrivaled only by the clergy.

If we compare youth in our study, ages 15-23, with other Americans of their age, we find them politically a bit more liberal. This shows up not only in their political preferences, but also in their attitudes toward certain societal restraints. But these differences are not great. They are typically American in their attitudes on most social issues.

From the few comparisons possible one is led to think of Lutheran youth as quite typical Americans except in three important areas: greater identification with their parents, more positive attitudes toward their congregation, and greater understanding of what makes the Christian faith distinctive.

Because of my interest in youth, I am attempting not only to understand what we found about Lutheran youth, but also to point the directions I see for ministry. I am attempting in this book to bridge the gap between that somewhat formal research report and an answer to the question, "So what—what does all this information mean in a local congregation?" And so I am writing here an interpretive report that is my understanding of what is required in a local youth ministry. Admittedly, it is not a "how to do it" book, but rather, one which presents a rationale for a way of looking at youth work.

I see a need for two major imperatives in a youth ministry—*mutuality* and *mission.* Youth of all subcultures need and want the warmth found in an accepting group. That is *mutuality.* Also, they need and want activities which give them a sense of purpose. That is *mission.*

This rationale—which forms the basis for my approach to ministry—has evolved out of previous studies, and A Study of Generations has underscored its soundness.

My theological orientation is Christian and my purpose is basically a pastoral one. I am writing to encourage an alliance in local congregations where youth and adults draw out the potential that is inherent in each other. Because this book is an interpretation and application of data, it is admittedly subjective. My biases are obvious and my understanding is limited.

One word of caution. This book is based on one kind of research data—self report. This means that we are limited in our knowledge of Lutherans to what they *said* they believe, value, and do.

Certainly I hope that young people will read this book. But I am writing it primarily for adults who work with youth, and most especially for parents. Mr. Ray Johnson, Youth Director of The American Lutheran Church, says it well when he describes parents as a congregation's "built-in youth ministers."

*Unrealistic stereotypes of youth distort adult
relationships with youth. Caricatures, in being
popularized, hinder communication between
generations with the result that fears compete
with trust. These caricatures encourage an age
prejudice within the church.*

PART ONE

Images Create Prejudices

Introduction

I would like to ask you to begin with a simple game.
Think of the phrase "today's youth." Now tell yourself what image flashes on the screen of your mind.
The parts of that "live picture" in your mind shape
rather powerfully how you as an individual relate to
young people. Suppose you become involved with a
group of them in a tense conflict situation. This can
happen easily no matter what your position in life
may be—teacher, pastor, parent, neighbor, businessman. Your "image" of today's youth will determine
how you react in that situation.

Data from A Study of Generations strengthen my
conviction that a major problem in youth work centers
in the negative image many adults hold of youth.
*Though youth hear the words of love and acceptance,
they feel the distrust and rejection of many whose
image of youth is a negative one.* If a youth's hair is

long or his behavior is part of the cultish response of his high school group, the inner feeling of many adults is one of anger and even total rejection.

When a person enters his teen years he inherits a public image that is distorted and negative—one that preconditions adult attitudes. Youth find this image reflected in the chance remarks of some adults, in the articles or pictures of mass media, and by the ways in which people in authority treat them. To most youth the negative image is an obvious fact; to most adults it is not so apparent.

Adults must take seriously the polarizing effects of negative images. Fear generated in adults and resentment built up in youth separate one from the other and reduce communication and trust. My purpose is to focus on these artificial barriers and show why such stereotypes ought to be challenged. False images are part of the darkness that truth can dispel. A basic tenet of our faith is that God has created all people in his own image to be loved and respected as Christ loves us. We must not, then, allow false and negative images to serve as artificial barriers to close relationships and feelings of mutuality between youth and adults.

Chapter 1

The Youth-Adult Gap

Generational struggle is a universal theme of history. As far back as Plato and Aristotle people were keenly aware of the conflict between generations. These men believed that the struggle between generations was essential for change in the political life of a nation. They believed that except for struggle, forms would remain unchanged and would fossilize. There is a need for tension between generations, they reasoned.

In writing about youth Aristotle made these characterizations: "Youth love honor and victory, they are fonder of their friends and companions than older men are, they have exalted notions because they have not learned life's necessary limitations, they think they can accomplish what others have not, their lives are regulated more by moral feeling than reasoning, they are ready to pity others."

Traditionally youth have been oriented to change, open to new ideas, less regulated by how things have been done in the past, and more inclined to upset the apple cart. They have always tended to press for new patterns and ways of doing things.

Traditionally, adults in positions of power have always been threatened by youth's idealism and their lack of realism in pressuring for changes. A hidden but real fear and resentment toward youth has been a natural result.

The threat youth pose for adults is intensified during times of social upheaval. As changes are begun by events in history the young people help to usher them in more quickly. Good illustrations of this are found in two well known periods in history—the Reformation and the Industrial Revolution. These two periods saw changes as drastic as those today and with these changes came open conflict between generations.

CONFLICT DURING THE REFORMATION

The days of Martin Luther knew concerns not limited to religious ones. No period in Western history until today saw the production of such massive literature on the problems of youth. Many writers took a dim view of youth's riotous conduct. Luther especially was embarrassed because youth were among the most active in promoting his reformation ideas. They used riots, violence, subversive action, and public disturbances to advance his cause. On one occasion when he met with them he got nowhere for he found them "hot with drink" and most unreasonable. When he preached about the evils of stirring up discontent, they accused him of joining the town council. These students, most of whom were teenagers, were convinced that Luther was dragging his feet. They wanted their mentor to condone their violence and give them more active leadership. To add a little pressure, some threatened to take his life.

You can imagine what the future looked like to the gray heads of Luther's day. In 1517 when Luther was the ripe old age of 34, nearly all of his followers were 30 years of age or younger. Conversely, most of his opponents at Wittenberg were 50 years old or older, some well over 70.

It would be hard to overestimate the contributions that have come to us out of this period of social change. Yet if we had lived then, we may well have despaired of the future.

CONFLICT DURING THE INDUSTRIAL REVOLUTION

Another analogue of today is the Industrial Revolution, 1760-1840. This period of social ferment is the time, according to Frank Musgrove, when both the steamboat and adolescence were invented. Previous to this time, young people were regarded as social inferiors and were classified with the servants who taught them. In 1789, someone complained that fathers knew their dogs better than their children.

You can imagine the changes in family life when the factories of the towns and cities opened their doors to child labor. Young people quickly took advantage of their opportunities for freedom. A 14-year-old could earn more money in a city factory than father could earn on the farm. This meant that youth of this age became free agents, living alone in the city and paying for their own food and clothing.

You can imagine, too, the youth population in some of those towns. In Kennedy of Manchester for instance, half of the 1020 working people were under 18 years of age. As you would surmise, this new adult status and freedom brought on youthful marriages. The peak percentage of early marriages reached in those days was not equalled until after World War II.

Before 1830 the English public schools for boys were known as places of safekeeping for potential revolutionaries and deviants. Well known places like Winchester, Rugby, and Eton were the scenes of repeated and ugly disturbances, settled only by the intervention of the English army.

Sensitive men of this time, such as Naismeth and Todd, much concerned about the ugliness of what was happening, entered the picture. They sparked vital youth movements which then caught on spontaneously near the end of the nineteenth century. Eight early forms of organizations developed for young people during that century, mostly devoted to young men: young men's unions, mechanics' institutes and mutual improvement societies, Sunday school classes, Sunday school teachers' meetings, singing schools, temperance societies, young people's missionary societies, and young people's devotional prayer meetings. Out of these beginnings came such youth organizations as the YMCA, Boy Scouts, church youth groups, and the Sunday school movement.

I remind you of these two periods not to imply that because "there is nothing new under the sun" we need not worry. Rather, I speak of these periods of social ferment, convinced that times of breaking out of old forms *can be* times of rebirth and renewal. In our day, neither complacency nor an emergency-crisis response is really helpful. What is required of us is imagination, openness, and a willingness to see our day, not only as one of change but of opportunity and challenge.

TOWARD THE YEAR 2000

Erik Erikson, a well known psychologist of youth, has looked ahead to the year 2000. It is his conviction that out of today's normlessness and seeming defiance of law, new boundaries will emerge, new ways of arriving at what is important in life. He believes that our ruthless heritage of radical enlightenment will force an important segment of our youth to be human without illusion, naked with narcissism, loving without idealization, ethical without moral passion, restless without being classifiably neurotic, and political without lying. In his opinion the nature of the social ferment will diminish the gap between generations, rather than widen the gap. These, of course, are conjectures. What is more to the point is his conviction that we are helping to determine the nature of youth in the year 2000 by the kinds of questions we now ask. These questions must lead not only to a better understanding of youth's behavior but also to a greater willingness to see the barriers which we as adults erect.

THE IMPORTANCE OF STANCE

If the stance which you as an adult take toward youth is a negative one, young people will sense it. They will feel on the defensive and react accordingly. It is quite safe to predict that you will not be comfortable in the presence of youth, or they with you. A gap will develop in communication and trust. This gap will serve only to encourage an age prejudice.

One's stance toward youth is highly related to one's stance toward life. Two major life orientations are identified in A Study of Generations—a law orientation and a gospel orientation. A law-oriented adult is more likely to look at life pessimistically and prejudge people. He is uncomfortable with anyone who "rocks the boat," and he is less given to helping people who are outside of his "ingroup." By virtue of his stance toward life, he is inclined to take a negative stance toward youth.

The gospel-oriented adult tends to view life and others positively, to accept and even welcome those who differ from him, and to be concerned for people who are hurting.

How you view young people is less a function of what they are like today, and more a function of how you view life. If you are oriented to rules, regulations, authority, then you are susceptible to a negative image. If you are oriented toward forgiveness, rebirth, and God's love, then the chances are that you hold a positive image.

This means that a very important factor in "bridging the gap" is that we who are adults "get our own heads on straight." It is the first step in narrowing the gap in trust and acceptance between generations. Contrariwise, the first step toward greater polarization between generations is to emphasize stricter rules as the solution to society's problems.

This book is no brief for peace and accord. A positive image of youth is not a prelude to "one big happy family." On the contrary, an openness to youth means that they will more readily express themselves and tell you what they don't like. We will become *more* aware of areas of tension rather than less.

Diversity and differences of opinion within the church must be accepted as normal and not abnormal. Our study has shown that of the many sources of diversity one of the most important is differences in age. We must allow for differences of opinion and give freedom within the life of the church for youth and adults to correct, inform, and challenge each other. But where in the life of our congregations is it possible for youth and adults to correct, inform, and challenge each other? The sensitivities of young people can serve as the conscience not only to society, but certainly also within the congregational fellowship.

18

Youth may not have the years of experience behind them, but they do have a peculiar insightfulness regarding some of the sham and pretense we as adults allow or take for granted. A Study of Generations has made it clear that youth do not feel this kind of freedom to speak, and that adults are not ready to welcome their ideas. Youth feel outside the decision-making and opinion-giving sector of their congregation.

Chapter 2

The Gap Can Be Bridged

During the 1960s, when the word *gap* was used to describe several statements of national concern (credibility gap, missile gap), it was also being attached to the word *generation*. Writers like Margaret Mead are making extreme claims about this gap. She expresses the conviction that we have entered a new age—an age so radically different from the past that people born prior to World War II should be considered "immigrants in time"; that is, they don't really belong to the present-day world, and they can't possibly understand it. In her view, the generation gap is a chasm between young and old people.

Other writers take less extreme positions. Theodore Roszak in *The Making of a Counter Culture* interprets the generation gap as a growing and ongoing separation. He compares it with the cleavage which first century Christians introduced into the culture of their day. As youth reject the Great Society, he says, they look for new expressions of community family patterns, esthetic forms, personal identities, ways of earning a livelihood, and sexual mores. He believes that the result will be a highly significant cultural change involving a new system of values for almost everyone.

Persons who agree with Mead and Rozak, interpreting the generation gap as a break in cultural values, view some of today's youth and students as a "new breed." They see them as new seeds in the soil of life, the harvest of which will furnish us with a new culture and a new life style.

CONTRASTING CLAIMS

Still other observers of youth and society deny that a radical break has occurred between generations. They do not interpret what is happening as a cultural break with the past. They point to history, insisting that there have always been groups for whom a strong generation gap has existed, and that these groups throughout history have been a definite minority. These observers point to the evidence of a close parent-child relationship for the majority of American youth today, and they suggest that generalizations about a generation gap are being made on the basis of what is true of only a minority of youth. In their view, this small minority of youth has been so over-publicized that they are seen as much more representative of youth than they really are.

By the early 1970s theorists of youth were making contrasting claims. Here are some of the most common theories and their opposite theories:

> *Some analysts speak of a "generation gap" so complete that it cannot be bridged.*
> Others deny its reality except for certain subcultures of youth.
> *Some believe that adolescence is a unique and stormy developmental period.*

21

Others know populations of youth that contradict the theory that youth must rebel.

Some believe that modern society is turning out conformist youngsters like a factory.

Others argue that modern society, rather than fostering homogeneity, is alienating youth from adult systems.

Some insist that we now have a universal youth culture and that youth are taking their signals primarily from their own age group.

Others question whether there is a youth culture by pointing out the similarities of youth and parents in values, beliefs, and behavior. External contrasts in dress, length of hair, and cultural interests are considered superficial and faddish rather than evidence of a true youth culture.

Some claim that the counter culture is the wave of the future and that people who live this way symbolize the youth of tomorrow.

Others agree that no subculture can be used to predict a trend in our pluralistic society. The life style of some, they say, may produce an opposite reaction among others. That is, a trend for one subculture of youth may produce an opposite trend for other subcultures.

Why these contrasting claims about youth? Why do scholars looking at the same events come to such different conclusions?

One reason relates to the academic background of each theorist. One's profession (whether sociology, psychology, anthropology, or history) inclines him to certain ways of understanding what happens in life. As a result, concrete events are forced into a pre-established theory. For example, sociologists tend to see "social forces" as *the* causes of youth discontent; psychologists see alienation or rebellion as *the* underlying cause; and anthropologists single out cultural factors. Each, true to his profession, tends to focus on some aspect of youth life which, though true, may be incomplete as an explanation.

Another reason for the contrasting theories is that some theorists use broadly based research for their claims whereas others generalize from very small and limited samples. Many of the commonly held convictions about today's youth are associated with such prominent names as Margaret Mead, Paul Goodman, Edgar Friedenberg, and Charles Reich. These are some of the people who contribute to "the literature of great ideas." But Douvan and Adelson in *The Adolescent Experience* observe that some of the great names in the social sciences, not finding scientific reports relevant to their concerns, have isolated themselves from broader facts and trends to the point of becoming eccentric. Jack Douglas even claims that men such as Friedenberg and Goodman give excellent documentation of their *lack* of experience with youth. They, as well as many other analysts, have evaded the world of youth and in its place have substituted merely their own understanding of youth.

In fairness it should be added that no theorist, including the one who draws on the findings of systematic research, has a balanced view of youth today. Each one interprets what he sees, not only through the glasses of his profession but also the eyes of his circle of friends. Reich, the economist, is undeniably influenced by the Yale students who helped him write his book. Margaret Mead, who studied youth in the Samoan Islands, cannot help but be impressed by the heady contrast between them and students on the Harvard campus. My interpretations are influenced by the youth I have worked with over three decades as youth director and campus pastor.

Because of this personal subjectivity, broad-scale research is essential. The findings are like a compass;

they help us reassess our direction. Or better yet, they are like an aerial view or map of a city; they help us gain a more balanced view of the entire youth population and see each section or subculture in relation or contrast to the other. Note the following research conclusions:

Youth's (ages 15-21) views on a broad range of social questions are remarkably moderate, even conservative. In sum, they describe a rather tolerant relaxed group whose attitudes and expectations on a great many subjects differ very little from their parents. Most youth listen to the rhetoric of dissent, pick what they want, then slowly weave it into the dominant social pattern (*Life*, Harris Survey, 1969).

Most empirical studies have consistently failed to demonstrate that adolescents and parents are at loggerheads and that there is a prevailing atmosphere of mutual disrespect, derogation, and disaffection as depicted in generation-conflict interpretations of adolescence (Weiner, 1967).

The majority of young people in a national sample does not fit the "generation gap" stereotype of rebellious youth casting aside the values of their elders. In fact, the dominant position they express essentially supports the status quo. But if this orthodoxy describes a majority of American youth, it is well to remember that a substantial minority—twenty percent or so—do dissent from the dominant position (Johnston and Bachman, 1971).

GENERATION GAP

The phrase "generation gap" is used to mean different things. Margaret Mead means a radical break between youth and adults in values, beliefs, life styles, attitudes, and in general, all communication. Others mean far less by the phrase. Some prefer rather to speak only of a communication gap or a social distance that needs to be bridged.

In A Study of Generations the claims of a radical break in values and beliefs between youth and adults were tested and found wanting. We measured generational differences on 52 dimensions and scales. (A scale consists of a group of items which focus on one specific *dimension* of values, beliefs, attitudes, opinions, or life styles.) Typical examples are these:

Humanity of Jesus (Belief)
Salvation by Works (Belief)
Feelings of Isolation and Pressure (Attitude)
Neighborliness (Life Style)
Questionable Personal Activities (Life Style)
Generalized Prejudice (Attitude)
Values of Self Development (Values)
A Personal Caring God (Belief)

Measures of these 52 dimensions make it possible to assess gaps between generations in what they believe and value, think and do. If World War II did in fact usher in a "new breed" (as some claim), it would be evidenced by glaring contrasts in what generations believe, what they consider important, what they think and do.

When we chart every dimension by generation (using the age groupings 15-29, 30-39, 40-49, and 50-65) we do not find a consistent radical break or contrast in values, beliefs, attitudes, opinions, or life styles. On the contrary, two-fifths of the dimensions show that youth and adults, for instance, give essentially the same answers. They identify similarly with their parents, are alike in their views of Christ's divinity, and value alike a controllable world.

On some dimensions, youth differ in their reports from those of middle-aged adults, but do resemble the oldest (ages 50-65). For instance, the young and old contrast with the middle-aged in these ways: more intense feelings of pessimism, greater desire for detachment from the world, and oddly, more widespread acceptance of the belief in salvation by works.

On most of the dimensions (three-fifths of them), however, there are significant contrasts between youth and adults. But there is no rupture that shows a radical break for the entire population of youth. The radical contrasts typify only some subcultures which, on the American scene and also in our sample, represent less than 20% of the population.

To summarize, the research evidence in A Study of Generations shows no universal or consistent break between generations. As other studies have shown, the generation gap as a universal phenomenon is a myth. The phrase must be reserved to describe the chasm which does exist between *some* youth and *some* adults. We are using it in this book to describe social distance—a gap in trust.

Have you ever wondered how past generations felt about their parents, how your parents and grandparents felt about their father or mother?

While it is true that comparisons between now and then are difficult, we do have something that is more than a guess. We have the results of how 5,000 persons (ages 15-65) answered items about their parents. They show the degree to which each person feels that he shares the same qualities as his parents.

The charting of scores on this set of items (Identification with Parents) is fascinating. The 39-40 year olds show the highest identification with their parents and the 64-65 year olds the lowest. Admittedly, memories dim and lose their preciseness. But when the oldest in our sample remember their parents, they recall as many dissimilarities in values and attitudes as do the

Study Guide
for

BRIDGING
THE
GAP

Study guide by David C. Wold

About the Guide and Its Use: Although this study guide addresses groups, individuals may find it helpful in (1) identifying the book's primary issues, and (2) providing a way of wrapping up what has been read.

Bridging the Gap deals with a subject appropriate for consideration by groups of adults or by cross-generational groups. Remember that it is important to be involved together in the discussion and sharing of insights.

The task of leadership may be shared or rotated, but someone within the group must act as discussion starter and coordinator. Though the leader may change, the leader's aim should be constant,

* to listen to the group's reactions and interpretations of the author's thought, to clarify and/or summarize;
* to make sure the group members take seriously the author's arguments while expressing their own opinions and reactions.

For the group's first meeting a leader should be designated--one who will have read the entire book and prepare to introduce it in an enthusiastic way, stimulating interest and curiosity.

PREFACE

Technical research reports seldom inspire wide readership. Even Lutherans may neglect *A Study of Generations*,* though the book is about them and contains insights potentially valuable for their expression of life and faith. In *Bridging the Gap* Strommen provides a wider audience easier access to the findings in *Generations*. He writes "to bridge the gap between that somewhat formal research report and an answer to the question, 'So what--what does all this information mean in a local congregation?'" Though *Generations* does not deal exclusively with youth, *Bridging the Gap* focuses on the data as it relates to "a rationale for a way of looking at youth work."

General Suggestions

The guide proposes five discussion periods (with the possibility of more). The plan for each session includes three elements:

Conversation. This provides opportunity for each participant to share insights or questions from his reading of the book. Conversation suggests dialog, not only with the author but also between persons present whose perceptions and feelings about the topic may vary widely. Though this will occupy a relatively brief portion of the period, it is nevertheless important to the development of the group. The group leader should note the questions raised or any patterns from the comments offered that may indicate where there is need to focus its study more intensively.

Concentration. This occupies the major block of time. The concentration is upon the book and the reader's reactions to it. This guide is meant to help focus our thoughts and reactions on the ideas of the author. Do not feel limited by the questions raised nor compelled to deal with all of them in any given session. Concentration suggests getting at the kernel of the writer's thought; and a good discipline is to attempt to distill the material under discussion into one or two clear sentences.

Contract. The group should make some commitments to itself. One commitment is to read the material to be discussed during the next session. There may be additional resources

---

* *A Study of Generations.* Merton P. Strommen, Milo L. Brekke, Ralph C. Underwager, Arthur L. Johnson. Minneapolis: Augsburg Publishing House, 1972. $12.50.

to be examined or textual data to be compared with findings in the local setting. The word *contract* should suggest that group members regard their involvement in these sessions as a commitment of both presence and preparation.

Setting

It is best to seat the group so that participants face and hear each other. This provides a less formal climate and should facilitate better discussion. Groups larger than ten persons should be subdivided into groups of four to six for the concentration section of the period. Each subgroup should report briefly to the whole group before dismissal so that unique or helpful insights may be shared.

You will need a copy of *A Study of Generations* as a resource. Check your local, church, or pastor's library; or order copies from Augsburg Publishing House. A "Summary of Findings" (pp. 286-304) will help orient the group to the background for the present book.

Suggestions for Each Session

The leader will profit from reviewing the general instructions carefully before each session, remembering that they are meant to be supportive and not restrictive.

THE CHANGING SCENE

Note: Do not distribute the book until instructed to do so in this session.

Conversation. Ask each member of the group to introduce himself, offering information that may help the group understand his perspective: i.e., married, have teenagers living at home, concerned about youth, etc. This is not meant to be clinical, just helpful. Have fun with your introductions.

Explain briefly the operational procedures suggested. If the group concurs, proceed. Stress that the leader's function is that of catalyst, not expert.

Concentration. Hand out copies of *Bridging the Gap*. Play the word association game (p. 11) in your group. What images form in your mind? List them. What similarities are there in the associations of people in the group? Do these suggest negative or positive experiences? Are the images based on personal experience? Others' impressions? From media reporting? Identify any images so negative that they may be barriers to relationship.

1) Read paragraph 2, page 7. Examine the copy of *A Study of Generations*. Read the first two paragraphs on page 8. Make your own clear statement of what Strommen says he is doing in this book.

2) The two major imperatives for youth ministry are articulated (p. 8) as mutuality and mission, perhaps new to you in this context. What content do you give these words?

3) When Strommen describes his intended audience (p. 9), do you see yourself as a "minister to youth"? How? Is that role new or foreign to you? Identify some public images that exist for youth in your community. Substantiate them or give evidence for their inaccuracy. Do you see yourself challenging stereotyping (p. 12)?

Contract. For the next time read pages 13-29. Jot down any strong impressions as you read. If you take issue with a statement, try to articulate your feelings and convictions. As you proceed continue to ask, What's the author's point? Is it valid? If so, then what?

THE GAP AND THE GOAL

Conversation. What overall impressions do you have from reading the first two chapters? Which statements or expressions were unclear? Observe who contributes freely to discussion and who appears hesitant. The more timid should be encouraged to participate without being pressured and the more verbal encouraged not to dominate and throttle wide participation.

Concentration.
1) What does the word *gap* suggest to you? Discuss whether it conveys an essentially positive or negative image.

2) What new insights did the historical overview of pages 13-16 provide for you? Discuss whether the author is justified in his hopeful statement that "times of breaking out of old forms can be times of rebirth and renewal" (p. 16).

3) How do you react to the statement (p. 17) that persons relate to youth as they relate to life in general?

4) Discuss what is a "law-oriented" or "gospel-oriented" person. (There are numerous references to this in *Generations*. Check the index.)

5) *Generations* found a significant number of Lutherans "law-oriented." Discuss whether this is a contributing factor to youth's not feeling free to speak (p. 19).

6) Read aloud the section (p. 24) that begins "Youth's views" and ends "dissent from the dominant position." What does this say to you? In what ways does it match your observations or contradict them?

7) Can you relate the following three statements? "Claims of a radical break...were tested and found wanting" (p. 25); "no universal or consistent break between generations" (p. 26); "chasm...does exist...a gap in trust" (p. 26).

8) "A realistic way to 'bridge the gap'" is described on pages 27-28. Recast the description in your own words. Reread the paragraph. Does this method sound realistic?

9) "The gap with which we need to be concerned is a gap in understanding, acceptance, trust, and communication" (p. 28). Explain why you do or do not accept that statement. What does this view mean to Lutherans whose traditional emphasis has been upon a ministry of Word and Sacrament?

Contract. For the next session read pages 30-47. Plan to talk with one youth or one adult (not in your group) this week. Ask how they view youth (if an adult) or how they think they are viewed (if a youth). Bring the results of your interviews to the next session.

DIFFERENT STROKES FOR DIFFERENT FOLKS

Conversation. Check out the results of the interviews. To what degree do they relate to observations in the text? Share your general observations from the reading. Ask yourselves if the group is increasing its capacity to share new ideas freely and to deal with differences of feeling and opinion expressed by members. In what way may this growth or lack of it relate to the material under discussion?

Concentration.

1) What is a "subculture" (p. 30)?

2) Read the section beginning "Unless youth" and concluding, "every wire service" (p. 32). Discuss whether this has been a factor in your community. In your congregation.

3) The author describes "peer-oriented" and "broadly-oriented" youth (pp. 34-36). What other names or "labels" would fit these classifications?

4) What is the author saying by including the historical perspectives on pages 38-39?

5) Seeing each person as "one of God's divine 'originals'" is a key to youth ministry and "bridging the gap" (pp. 37-40). What theological conviction undergirds that statement? What biblical support is there for such a posture?

6) Reference is made to *The Greening of America* (p. 41) and to three conflicting world views (pp. 42-43). The author does not "buy" the descriptions without reservation but nevertheless regards them seriously, concluding, "There does appear to be a subtle but real shift in mood or consciousness" (p. 43). Can you accept that statement? Or does this appear to be using history to prove a preset conclusion?

7) In the conclusion (beginning p. 44), the author uses the words *feel* or *feeling* several times. What is the significance of this? If you accept these feelings, what relevance do they have to "youth ministry"?

Contract. The reading assignment is pages 47-72. Think about your congregation and the term *renewal:* where should renewal take place in the ministry for and with youth?

LONELINESS AND THE NEED FOR RENEWAL

Conversation. Where have members of the group "been" in their thinking this past week? What are the ways in which this study has begun to affect your thinking processes? Discuss thoughts from the last session that have made a difference to people.

Concentration.

1) "To feel loved and accepted by people is vital to feeling loved and accepted by God" (p. 50). What is your reaction to that statement? Can we equate "feeling loved" with "being loved"? What is the relationship of Authority of the Word and "feeling loved and accepted by God"?

2) "One obvious need is for groups where there is close, warm interaction" (p. 52). What does this say about our present models for youth ministry?

3) Two out of five Lutherans "are strongly oriented to the law...live a practical atheism...[believe in] salvation by works" (p. 54-55). Address this from a gospel perspective. What does the gospel enable us to do in light of this learning about ourselves? Identify any gospel priorities that seem to emerge for our ministry.

4) The author suggests that our reflections about "youth and their sense of aloneness from God" (p. 57) is part of a larger issue. What is the larger issue?

5) "Feelings are important" (p. 59). How are feelings regarded in this parish? Are they part of our concern or is our communication of faith seen apart from feelings?

6) What content do the concepts *transcendence* and *immanence* (p. 64) have for you as adults? What is the author's point?

7) Youth want to "experience the gospel as well as hear the words" (p. 65). How can the Christian community address itself to that need?

8) Do P.E.T. and P.A.C.T (p. 69) sound like helpful resources? (Are they available in your community?) Discuss whether communication is an end in itself.

9) Deal with the task of where and how effective youth work (pp. 70-71) can begin in your parish.

Contract. If the author's words have validity, think of their meaning for your own parish. As you read pages 72-101, begin to write down the priorities for youth ministry in your parish. Reread portions of the book: how do they relate to the last two chapters (esp. pp. 8; 18 "where in the life of our congregations"; 40 "goals of a congregational youth ministry"; 48 "at the heart of a sense of alienation"; 55-57 "Need for Renewal"; 61-62 supportive fellowship and "lover's quarrel"; 65 a desire to "*experience* the Gospel")?

MUTUALITY AND MISSION

Conversation. Share what you see of patterns of thought or interrelatedness in the last chapters of the book and portions read earlier. What central theme or themes is the author developing? Summarize in a sentence or two the heart of his thought as you understand it.

Concentration. On pages 75-77 the author develops the thesis that what is needed by youth is "a sense of family."

1) Is he talking about a real family? What are the characteristics of such a family? What does mutuality mean in the setting of a family?

2) On page 75 the "first essential in a youth ministry" is noted. Relate that section to pages 78-80. What are "non-experts" (p. 78)? If "technique" (p. 79) is not the key, what kind of strategy can we have for an honest and effective youth ministry?

3) What is meant by "ordinary people...free to open their lives to others" (p. 79)?

4) Discuss whether the "mutual exchange" model for youth ministry is healthy or simply a case of the blind leading the blind. Is this style a "cop-out" from authority and responsibility or is it the ultimate fulfillment?

5) What implications do you see for this model beyond "youth ministry" in a congregation?

6) "Youth and adults have a mutual ministry to each other" (p. 83). Relate this to the statement on page 82 about "intergenerational life-style."

7) Pages 85-87 discuss "guidelines that help establish a congenial climate." How do these relate to the theme of the chapter? Do they sound like "techniques" or "stances"?

8) A discussion of the importance of "sense of purposefulness" and some impediments to "mission" is found on pages 88-92. (Note particularly p. 89, the two basic features that undermine any "sense of mission.") Can you relate that to the findings that forty percent of Lutherans are law-oriented? What does the gospel say to this "heresy" (p. 89)?

9) Some signs of hope are noted on page 95: "Youth are as willing to serve as are adults of middle age." How willing are those adults? What are the risks when youth get involved in "mission"? What is your opinion about their conviction (p. 96) "that far too little has been done in becoming involved in social issues"?

10) Is the "make-believe church" (p. 97) a viable alternative to full partnership in mission?

Contract. "Life demands commitment" (p. 98). What commitments do you see emerging from this study? What issues have been raised that call for your involvement? Decide if the group should negotiate a new contract. If not, what are the dimensions of the continuing task? How is *Bridging the Gap* a stance for our ministry?

Code No. 10-0901

more critical 15-16 year olds. Feelings of distance between youth and parents may have been as great for youth at the turn of the century as they are today.

Supporting evidence is found in Hill's book, *Family Development in Three Generations,* that reports a study of grandparent, parent, and young-married generations of 100 families. After examining comparative data on location of residence, degree of education, husband-wife and parent-child relationships, plans and plan fulfillment and beliefs on child-rearing, he finds that discontinuity (a "generation gap") was apparent between the grandparent and parent generations, rather than between parent and young marrieds.

In A Study of Generations, we also tested Margaret Mead's claims as stated in her book, *Culture and Commitment.* What did we find?

The idea of a radical break in values and beliefs between youth and adults finds no support in the data on youth and adults in A Study of Generations. Nor are Mead's typologies (three different kinds of culture) useful in classifying Lutherans. Rather, they identify three points of view that co-exist in all ages. Some people cling to the past and are strongly oriented to the status quo; and others, close to one in five (18%), are ready for serious change. The majority are committed to a process of reassessment that involves the past and the present—youth working with adults—in meeting the problems of the future.

It appears that in the voluntary setting of a congregation, a collaborative model is fostered, where adults collaborate with youth in partnerships on boards, projects or services. Modeling (where one serves as an example for another) is encouraged as youth learn from each other and from adults. Likewise adults learn from each other and from youth. As each identifies with the other in an atmosphere of congeniality and mutuality, the prevailing attitudes and beliefs are adopted. Such interaction and mutual sharing is a unique strength in a congregational fellowship that ought to be encouraged. It counteracts polarization and works against an age prejudice. It is a realistic way to "bridge the gap."

CONCLUSIONS

Research findings from many quarters converge on the same conclusions. There is little evidence of a break between generations for about 80% of the youth in our sample. The majority of this country's youth are following the patterns established by their parents—whether good or bad. Most research studies deny that youth have a unique set of values and attitudes. Youth and adults of a given community reflect approximately the same array of values.

We still have the problem of ruptured homes. Our concern must increase for parents whose style of interaction with their children and the values they champion have led the youth to reject their parents. Also, we have the growing minority of youth who live in worlds that are "poles apart" from their parents. For ideological reasons many youth evidence a separation that following Christ often creates between parents and youth.

We are not faced with a fearsome invisible barrier unique to this electronic age. We are facing barriers which our parents and grandparents had to struggle through to which the age-old solutions of acceptance and bridge-building still apply. Human nature has not changed and neither has its proneness toward polarization and alienation.

The gap with which we need to be concerned is a gap in understanding, acceptance, trust, and communication. It is a gap in sensitivity and perception as each age group sees life through different world views. What is foreign to a ministry of reconciliation is an unwillingness by both youth and adults to narrow this gap. What is redeeming is to believe that "in Christ there is neither Jew nor Gentile, male nor female," youth nor adult.

Chapter 3

Contrasting Youth Cultures

Subcultures are collections of persons who interrelate through shared experiences and activities. These subcultures reflect their identity through similar values, beliefs, opinions, and life styles. There is not one youth subculture, but many, each contrasting with the others.

When we make generalizations about all youth, based on information on only one subculture, we are in trouble. What may be true for one subculture may be false for another, just as what may be true for one person may not be true for another. Not all are heading in the same direction, or toward the same end in our society. On the contrary, the highly publicized activities of one subculture are often a source of dismay and anger to the youth of another subculture.

MASS MEDIA DISTORTIONS

One cannot ignore the impact of mass media on the consciousness of all Americans and their effect in establishing a negative image. The youth stories selected to appear on television or radio, or to headline newspapers and magazines, are stories that favor certain subcultures. In featuring the extreme groups, mass media have helped establish a national mind-set. They have provided images for public thought which give the impression that all youth are like the few.

When "news" favors the bizarre, tragic, grotesque, or shocking, the outcome is predictable. The youth emblazoned on the public's mind will be the extremists, the rebels, and the avant-garde.

It is a matter of record that radical and alienated youth get wide press coverage. During the late 1960s and early 1970s we were bombarded with articles about the Woodstock syndrome (a passive subculture shaped by rock music and drugs), political protestors (ranging from the violent Weathermen to moderate political activists), communes (from communal living in New Mexico to encounter groups at Big Sur), the occult advocates (searching for meaning through astrology, Tarot cards, I Ching, and varieties of meditation), and Jesus Freaks (who have turned from drugs to Jesus experiences and Puritan fervor). Images of such youth continuously appearing on television or in the press can only distort the way adults see youth.

A comprehensive review of national studies on youth and students between 1964 and 1970, They'd Rather Be Left, takes special note of the tendency of youth, as well as adults, to overestimate anything that is dramatic. For example, when youth in a 1971 national survey were asked to estimate the percent of their own age group who have tried drugs, two-thirds guessed 50% or more and one-third estimated 70%. Yet a study of these same students showed that no more than one-third had ever had any experience with a drug (Lipset and Schaflander, 1972).

Fifteen years ago adults worried about young people

and their involvement with sex as they worry today about youth's involvement with drugs. Because sex escapades made the news as drugs now command the headlines, adults held exaggerated ideas about what young people were doing when alone on a date. This distortion came through clearly in our studies of Lutheran youth in 1959. We asked adults to answer the survey items "as they thought the young people were answering them." The area adults grossly exaggerated was youth's involvement in dating problems. Of the 18 problem areas that were surveyed, none showed greater differences between what the youth reported and what the adults estimated. We found, for instance, that not more than one of two youth were troubled by these matters. One obvious reason was that one of two seldom if ever had dates. About a fourth of the boys were bothered because they were "not interested in dating" and assumed they should have been. And yet adults thought dating was a big problem for the majority. We now have a parallel situation in adult concern over drug use among youth.

Not much has been written on youth's accomplishments to offset the destructive activities of the most alienated youth. Unless youth do what is bizarre, unconventional, shocking, revolutionary, controversial, tragic, or frightening, their lives lack news interest. A young person can visit a nursing home each week and bring joy and hope to some forgotten citizens without breaking into print. But let him strike an octogenarian and rob him of his purse or life and the account will be featured on the daily newscast and carried over every wire service.

HOW YOUTH DIFFER

To be aware of the variety of subcultures among youth is to realize that youth cannot be caricatured.

Even in looking at subcultures, however, remember that though groups of youth are alike in some ways, there are other ways in which no one is alike. Each person has his individuality and therefore never can be classified and labeled. Nor am I attempting to do this here. Rather I am describing how *groups* of youth may differ. To impose on youth in general an image of rebelliousness and basic antagonism, for example, when that image applies only to a minority, is not true. If we hold such a stereotype, we antagonize youth and reduce our own sensitivity to them.

Cooperative Culture and Contra-Culture

Jack Douglas classifies youth on the basis of their attitude toward adults. Using this as our criterion we can speak of two distinct subcultures—a "Cooperative Culture" and a "Contra-Culture." One group cooperates with the adult society, while the other group acts without regard for adults, or against them. Admittedly, youth in either group may be co-opted youth, that is, youth who are manipulated into cooperating with adults or into opposing them.

Most youth cooperate with adults. These youth of the Cooperative Culture belong to such organizations as Boy Scouts and Girl Scouts, church youth groups, Y.M.C.A. and Y.W.C.A., athletic associations, business opportunity groups, and farm youth organizations such as 4-H. They generally cooperate with their adult teachers and see themselves as adults-in-the-becoming. These, the majority, are sometimes known as "straight youth."

Youth in the Contra-Culture have a predominantly antagonistic view of life and are given the widest attention. They also subdivide into two groups: those with a "troublemaking" or "tough" orientation, and those who reject the "square" world and set up an alternative way of life.

The first group is closely associated with the urban lower class and is found especially within certain ethnic groups. Though "troublemakers," these youth usually do not act out of their rebellion against the adult world, but rather against their own age group through gang warfare.

The others focus on their own entertainment (such as motorcycling or surfing) or on forming life styles. They basically reject the work-a-day world and idealize the values of leisure, feeling, and idealism. Their rebellion is expressed in "not doing," in "not working," in "not being rational," and in "not being part" of any organized group. Drugs are typically a part of these Contra-Cultures, though in lesser degree drugs are also used by youth of the Cooperative groups.

Peer-Oriented and Broadly-Oriented Youth

Another way of classifying youth is to use the way they relate to people of various age groups. Some youth can relate only to their own age group (Peer-Oriented), whereas others can relate to and enjoy people of all ages (Broadly-Oriented). Still others can relate only to older people. They can be called "little adults." As yet we have no data on this sub-culture.

A number of doctoral studies in 1968 and 1969 identified these two kinds of high school youth—Peer-Oriented and Broadly-Oriented. These studies indicated that Peer-Oriented youth could be described by one or more of the following characteristics:

—come from emotionally destructive homes
—shun participation in formal organized activities

—lack commitment to any ideology
—reflect various feelings of alienation
—are involved in alcohol, drugs, and questionable activities
—use the peer group to compensate for what they do not get in their homes.

A positive characteristic of Peer-Oriented youth is their greater willingness to take risks—to be adventuresome. Some, as revolutionaries, have helped bring about needed reforms in their school and community.

The Broadly-Oriented youth show one or more of these characteristics:

—active in school, church, and community organizations
—achieve higher grades
—more popular in school
—more active in school leadership positions
—come from congenial homes
—report a good relationship with their father

A negative characteristic of the Broadly-Oriented youth is their proneness to be tolerant of the status quo and their greater willingness to learn the rules of conformity.

A Study of Generations showed that high school youth array themselves along a continuum with being Peer-Oriented at one end and Broadly-Oriented at the other. Within Lutheran congregations, about one-fifth are primarily Peer-Oriented. Distinguishing characteristics of these youth are:

—high distrust of adults
—high involvement in questionable activities
—strong identification with the drug culture
—strong criticisms of the church

These are broad generalizations and should not be used as pigeon holes to classify youth. Though a high correlation is established between criticism and personal adjustment, this does not mean that their criticism is not valid or that all criticism is an expression of a distressed person. For example, a youth's commitment to an ideology may lead him to criticize his church. Such criticisms may not reflect a cynical view of life but rather the expression of an enlightened conscience. His Amos-like denunciation of pretense and smugness may be what is needed.

Lest the characterizations suggest that broadly-oriented or status quo youth are the "good kids" let me add this comment. There are broadly-oriented youth who have simply learned how to play the game of "getting ahead." They do no more than respond to the wishes of their group and already could be called "Archie Bunkers." They need to interact with youth who have come to know "grace."

Non-College Youth

The large majority of American youth do not go to college, yet we hear little about this group. For that reason, the data from a study of 2,881 non-college youth and 723 college youth, Thornburg's *Contemporary Adolescence,* is important.

This national cross-section of American young adults showed that attitudes and opinions of non-college young adults are quite different from those of college students. The life style of non-college youth is so much like that of their parents that, applied to them, the idea of a "generation gap" is a myth. Compared with college students they are more conservative, more prone to having traditional values, more religious, more respectful, more work-oriented, more money-oriented, more patriotic, more concerned about moral living, more conforming, more accepting of the draft and war, less activism-oriented, less sympathetic with activists, less drug prone, and less permissive in sexual activity.

Students

Because radical students have claimed front-page coverage, it is easy to forget that there are subcultures within the student population. Lionel Lewis tested and found valid a classification that distinguishes between four types of college students:

Academic	Students who identify with ideas and with their school
Collegiate	Students who do not identify with ideas but do identify with their school
Nonconformist	Students who identify with ideas but not with their school
Job-Oriented	Students who do not identify with either ideas or with their school

Students in the Collegiate and Job-Oriented subcultures have few, if any, intellectual goals and do not generally associate with those who might help them develop intellectual values. Students in the Academic subculture, interestingly, rank well above the others in humanitarian concerns.

In his study, Lewis notes a decrease in the Collegiate subculture following World War II (a decrease in the importance of fraternities, sororities, and extracurricular activities). A shift occurred toward an increase in the Nonconformist subculture (such as militant protest organizations) and the Job-Oriented subculture. In other words, the big shift was away from the type of students who identify with their school and toward students who do not.

37

The Nonconformist Subcultures

Even the much publicized nonconformist students can be subdivided into contrasting groups. Here I make reference to protesting student groups of the late 1960s. Moynihan singles out two different kinds of protest behavior and identifies groups in early history that acted similarly.

He notes that some students, people of vision, are committed to sharing another's fate and helping him shape his destiny. These students are conscious of people who are cut off from the resources of power. Moynihan compares these protesters to the outrageous young people who lived Christianity in second-century Rome. Their society played in the lecture room with the concepts of moral good and evil, but ignored them in the arena of life.

How were the early Christians evaluated? It was said of them that they were "bad citizens," refusing public employment and avoiding service in the army. They had no temples, no altars, no images and boasted just that. They had little interest in respectable people who observed the rules of society and tried to keep it running; they cared only for the outcast and miserable. They were in the minds and word of Celsus, "altogether of a seditious and revolutionary character."

Without question, some youth speak to the rational, tolerant, and reasonable society of today with the same irrationality, intolerance, and unreasonableness of youth in the second century. In a sense they are alienated youth. They stand in opposition to the values and injustices of our society. Theirs is an ideological alienation.

A second group of protesting youth knows an alienation that is not "for" but "from" society. Theirs basically is a rejection of religion and its laws; their standards of conduct are derived wholly from internal personal resources. Among the most visible of these groups are the bearded and the sandaled ones who in the words of Moynihan, "live on air, love, and alas drugs." They too have their counterpart in history, the Brethren of the Free Spirit. These people permeated vast areas of medieval Europe from the 11th century and on, almost to our own time. Theirs was both a mystical craving for an immediate experience of God and a search for the erotic. They denounced marriage as an impure state and practiced sexual promiscuity as a matter of principle. When wealth appeared in Europe, these Brethren preached a communism of property and chose to be utterly penniless.

CONCLUSION

It cannot be assumed that attitudes and practices of nonconformist college students typify all young adults or all youth. Neither can it be assumed that the distrust of Peer-Oriented youth characterizes all high school youth. Such generalizations are a disservice because they encourage unrealistic stereotypes that are an offense to many youth.

Having shown how youth differ by groups, let me quickly say that generalizations about subgroups are to be used for understanding and not for labelling and classifying youth. It is one thing to be alert to characteristics often found among peer-oriented youth and another thing to assume that every peer-oriented person has all the characteristics or even most of them. It is vital that we see each person as a unique individual who combines in himself a mixture of qualities that defy classification. Each person needs to be seen as one of God's divine "originals" and, like a painting, is to be enjoyed for his uniqueness. Seeing youth as people and as individuals of priceless worth is basic to "bridging the gap." This is one of the goals of a con- gregational youth ministry. Mass media images of youth must not be allowed to erect walls between youth and adults.

Chapter 4

There Is a Shift in Mood

It may seem that I am ignoring the prophetic voices of today and dismissing their contribution in cavalier fashion. It may seem also that I am ignoring the dramatic rise of the counter culture, drug usage, communal living, and all the portents of momentous change. It can rightfully be argued that significance is not always contained in the size of percentages but in the possible impact of a minority group. In other words, what appears to be a cloud no larger than the size of a man's hand may be, in reality, an advance notice of a storm of revolutionary proportions.

A SHIFT IN WORLD VIEWS

Charles Reich, in *The Greening of America,* advances this point of view. He contends that the youth of the counter culture embody a world view that promises to spread and become a revolutionary force that will be accepted by adults as well as youth. He concludes

41

that one can expect marked changes in the structure of society and the educational approach of school and church.

Reich's thesis is not based on a radical break between youth and adults (as is true of Mead's thesis). He contends, rather, that the growing tension between youth and adults is based on three conflicting world views that are not exclusively held by any one age group. Reich's book is much criticized, and perhaps rightly so. But in my opinion he has made a major contribution in his description of these three world views—Consciousness I, Consciousness II, and Consciousness III. I find these descriptions to a considerable extent supported by our data.

Consciousness I is the world view that characterizes the American farmer, small businessman, or worker of the pre-World War I days. For these people the goal in life was success in the competition of life where hard work, self-denial, character, and morality were the winning ingredients. In this world view, competition is seen as the law of man and of nature; life is basically the harsh pursuit of self-interest; production, invention, and achievement are the symbols of progress.

Underlying Consciousness I is a conviction that social problems are traceable to bad character, and that the least government is the best government.

Consciousness II is a world view that found its impetus and rise during the 1930s and '40s and became dominant in the early '50s. The thesis is that man is aggressive and needs to be contained by law. It holds that control by a central authority is essential. This implies that society is best when it is planned, organized, rational, and administered. It follows that the focus must be on the common good of the group, with

42

clearcut standards and an emphasis on ability and achievement through the organization.

Consciousness III is a reaction against Consciousness II. It is a reaction against the logical, disciplined, and controlled approaches which characterize that period. It is a reaction against standards in favor of freedom from restraint. Consciousness III seeks to recover the individual who is lost in the group emphasis of Consciousness II. It instead exalts genuine relationships as the highest value in life and rejects the idea of evaluating people and imposing standards on them. This world view encourages commitment to the welfare of other persons and welcomes experiences which awaken the dulled spirit.

Reich believes that these three world views have arisen during identifiable periods of national life. Yet one can point out that Consciousness II has always been more characteristic of adults, and Consciousness III has always been more characteristic of youth. Adults tend to be associated with tradition, standards, organization, conformity, and regulations. Youth, on the other hand, tend to be associated with creativity, new forms, new styles of life, and change.

It does not seem, however, that today's shift in consciousness among both youth and adults can be explained away as something which has been traditionally with us. There does appear to be a subtle but real shift in mood or consciousness. Because of this shift, we are faced with a need to make changes within our structures, changes which acknowledge the contribution of a Consciousness III and reflect an awareness of its feeling tone. This shift in consciousness seems to be felt by most people, adults as well as youth. And this may be why some of the wildest claims about youth gain a hearing.

A SHIFT IN VALUES

Roszak's analysis in *The Making of a Counter Culture* differs from Reich in several respects. When he talks about a counter culture, he excludes many groups and many practices that Reich includes. Reich calls "living off the fat of the land" a non-career. But Roszak does not applaud the spoiled middle-class young who think that being human has something to do with fun and games. He decries the 17-year-old who, in leaving the comfortable bosom of a middle-class family to become a beggar, thinks he is making a formidable gesture of dissent. Neither does Roszak's hope for the future include the Bohemian fringe of the disaffected youth culture that seeks a pharmacological panacea for the ills of life. Rather, he believes that a small group of thoughtful youth is creating a change in values similar to the one in the second century when Christians introduced a new way of life into their culture. He sees a growing reaction to the science-dominated technocracy of our day, and with it a defection from an intellectuality that looks for a technical solution, to all problems.

CONCLUSION

There is a feeling of disaffection among youth, a feeling of being alone and of being loosed from their moorings. Over half are troubled by feelings of isolation and a sense of being out of touch with God and man. They cry for the personal touch and they revolt against the cold and structure-bound attitudes of Consciousness II. They do not want the perfect liturgical service; rather they want someone to reach out and touch them. They want a transcendent God who sits next to them and says, "I love you." They want human

44

lips and hearts to make incarnate how God thinks and feels towards them.

What has been said in this chapter about a shift in mood might have been said 50 or 5000 years ago. However, the attitudes and feelings that typify Consciousness III seem stronger now. There seems to be a reaction away from the highly organized to the more person-centered approach. Many adults join the youth in preferring:

a new emphasis on "being" rather than "doing"
a greater accent on feelings and experience
a desire for more opportunities to know one another in depth
greater sensitivity for suffering persons
greater interest in variety and experimentation

There seems to be a growing disenchantment with the promises of the expert and a reaching out to powers that are beyond mankind. There is a disenchantment with the idea that man can solve every problem in life by analysis and research-based solutions.

One of the shifts in mood is a heightened sense of "being out of touch" with others. This feeling of aloneness shows itself in what youth have to say about God, their church, and adults. The walls erected by adult images or prejudices serve only to increase the aloneness.

PART TWO

Walls Increase Loneliness

Introduction

Alienation can be described in two ways. First, it can be considered unidimensional—having one dimension; that is, a quality of life which is common to all people. In each of us there is a degree of estrangement from ourselves, our fellowman, our God. We often sense that we are "out of touch" with someone else. This sense of alienation may, like any chasm, widen and deepen. Or it may narrow at times—times when we sense we are very much "in touch" with ourselves, with others, with God. Briefly, then, the unidimensional aspect of alienation is an aloneness which every person experiences to some degree.

A second way of describing alienation is based on the scientific evidence that alienation has many dimensions—is multidimensional. Each dimension is a feeling tone which, though distinct from the others, alienates a person from somebody or something. These dimensions are usually labeled powerlessness, normlessness, psychic isolation, self-estrangement, and meaninglessness. Though alienation expresses itself in this variety of forms, at the heart of a sense of alienation is distrust of others. It is an inability to entrust oneself to anyone, to commit oneself to any person or cause, an inability to see the trustworthiness of another. Contacts with people are only for the purpose of using them. Other expressions of alienation are pessimism, hostility, self-contempt, and the feeling of being an outsider. To an alienated person life and the universe appear unstructured, the future seems bleak. This feeling tone is one which we must acknowledge as a fact of life and recognize as a shaping influence in the lives of many people in every society. However, among the youth of today, extreme forms of aloneness are seen more frequently than in the past.

Using the data of A Study of Generations, we can examine some of the specific aspects of alienation, all the while asking ourselves these questions: Who are the most alienated youth? How is their alienation expressed? What factors are most strongly linked to these feelings? What proportions of youth are affected, and in what ways?

Chapter 5

The Chilling Effects of Aloneness from God

What contributes most to youth's feelings of alone-ness and alienation from God?

Our data show that young people (ages 15-23) who are most anxious about their uncertain relationship with God have two major characteristics. The first is a sense of isolation from people and feeling under pressure. Typical expressions are these:

> I often feel as if it would be good to get away from it all.
>
> There are so many problems to deal with today that sometimes I could just "blow up."
>
> I often feel left out of things that are going on around here.
>
> I feel all alone in the world fairly often.

A second major characteristic of youth alienated from God is a sense that life has no meaning. These youth lack a sense of purpose and look at life with feelings of despair. For them life is empty. If you talk with them privately you may hear variations of these themes:

> In thinking of my life I often wonder why I exist.
> My life is empty, filled only with despair.
> I have discovered no mission or purpose in life.
> Facing my daily tasks is a painful and boring experience.

FEELINGS OF ISOLATION AND PRESSURE

Who among the youth of a congregation tend to feel most isolated and under pressure?

Of the many possibilities considered, family happiness and age emerge as the ones most prominently associated with feelings of isolation. This shows how strongly a young person's feelings about God interrelate with the quality of his family life and with his sense of being accepted in some group. To feel loved and accepted by people is vital to feeling loved and accepted by God.

When we study the youth who feel most isolated and under pressure, we discover that they are among the most critical of their church, the most conscious of many things they dislike in their congregation. This undercurrent of feeling also colors their attitude toward school and work. Life, whether at school or work, is disappointing and empty of meaning.

Those caught in this isolation are easily hurt by criticism. They find it hard to carry on a conversation, assuming that others think poorly of them. As a protection they frequently make use of a "front." Though concealed and protected by this "front" they still feel isolated and lonely. And unfortunately this isolation is seldom overcome at a church youth meeting. I say this because of what our studies have revealed.

This feeling of isolation and pressure, is, of course,

not unique to church youth. A 20-year longitudinal study of young men entering an Eastern college (Haverford) shows the same evidences of alienation (Heath, 1968). It is seen in the ways these young men are coping with the increasing strains and pressures of college life. Three trends were reported. One trend is an increasing inhibition and intellectualized control of impulses and emotions. The goal is to become cool, suave, sophisticated, and to have control of oneself. It is the image of the cool kid trying to isolate himself from much of what is warm and tender within him.

A second trend is an increasing self-centeredness that includes an overevaluation of one's importance, especially one's intellectual powers. This trend is at the expense of valuing a religious way of life that calls for commitment to some external meaning or belief, to a conviction that there is a source of power on whom he must lean.

The third trend relates directly to self-estrangement. There is an evident decline in strength of human and social ties as evidenced by heightened individualism, alienation, loneliness, and social incompetence. A striking illustration of this estrangement is seen in the percentage of students who respond to a certain type of item. Take for instance the item, "I could be happy all alone in a cabin in the woods or mountains." In 1948, 23% said "yes" to this item, whereas 20 years later, in 1967, the percentage had risen to 45%. Another illustration: "At parties I am more likely to sit by myself or with just one other person than to join in with the crowd." In 1948 there were 23% who said "yes," and by 1967 the percentage had more than doubled. Heath, who carried out this 20-year study, asks the question, "What is the consequence of this growing estrangement?" His one word answer is "loneliness."

How can we best meet this feeling of loneliness in the teen years? One obvious need is for groups where there is close, warm interaction. Lonely youth need persons who will convey to them personally the helping relationship that they need. One essential in any youth program is the mutuality and close interaction of a caring community. In our studies of youth groups we find that mere camaraderie and fun do not minister to the feeling of aloneness. Young people will say their youth groups rank high when it comes to this item: "We have a lot of fun and good times." But their lowest rank of 40 items is for the one that says: "I feel free in my group to talk about the deep and personal things of my life."

This need for mutuality is even stronger in our day when the high winds of alienation increase their chilling effect. Congregations and schools must acknowledge the importance of feelings and the necessity of a warm emotional climate. Aloneness from God is linked undeniably with aloneness from man. That is why the walls of prejudice serve to heighten the loneliness of the ones prejudged.

FEELINGS OF PURPOSELESSNESS

Youth most devoid of a sense of purpose are pessimistic about life, and, therefore, expect nothing good from the future. They are alienated from hope. Having turned in on themselves they quite easily become preoccupied with their own interests and advantage. They reject the idea of living for others and for God and come to see Christianity as something you exploit for your own advantage. You can expect a pessimistic young person to reflect attitudes like these:

> A person must look out for himself since there is no one else to depend on for help.

>   There is little one person can do to make the
>   world a better place in which to live.
>   To get ahead today you sometimes have to be bad
>   as well as good.

Our analysis of reports from the *most* pessimistic
youth shows these characteristics. More of them are
males, anti-church, unwilling to accept changes, oriented to salvation by works, and the least accepting of
religious values. Furthermore, they are disappointed in
their church and least willing to affirm a faith. Theirs
is a malady or defect of faith commonly seen in today's society.

Schofield, in his book *Psychotherapy, the Purchase
of Friendship,* comments on maladies found outside the
realm of the mental health professions. One of these
he calls a "pseudo-neurosis," or defect of faith. He
believes that when the faith of man is in a state of
fever or deterioration, the result is unhappiness. Because man was created for faith, alienation from God
is an unnatural state. Hence, a pastor or representative
of the faith is needed to help the person find a living
faith.

We are speaking of an alienation that touches all
men. In a real sense, commitment and alienation exist
side by side for all people in the same way as faith and
doubt coexist. Just as our inclination to alienate ourselves from God requires that we counteract by re-
newed commitment, so doubt stimulates faith to search
for new mental images. In this tension we find life. As
we know so well, doubt and faith often reverse their
positions for many young people. What some youth
formerly believed they now doubt; and, what previous-
ly was doubt, they now affirm as true. But even for
youth who believe in their doubts, a longing remains.
There is still the nagging doubt that maybe there is a
moral order; maybe there is a God with whom they

must come to terms. Because most American youth acknowledge the reality of God, their alienation is a conscious estrangement.

Stewart, in his book *Adolescent Religion,* tells about two separate evaluations of his sample of 60 youth. The psychiatrist who interviewed them said, "I've interviewed 40 of the young people in your sample and I can tell you that they are only institutionalists and conformists. With one or two exceptions they have not experienced a first hand struggle with the religious realities of sin, guilt, forgiveness, faith, commitment. They are living on values fed them by their parents such as 'don't stick your neck out,' 'don't rat on a friend,' 'obey the rules while the boss is around.' "

The psychologist who also interviewed them said much the same. After assessing 30 youth he said, "I find that they know the words but not the music of religion. They are uninfluenced by it. They take their values from the peer group." Stewart found that though this was generally true, a minority could be called truly religious. For them faith is an intensely meaningful thing. The same is true for youth in A Study of Generations. About one in four know a personal, caring God and reflect a positive attitude toward life and death.

The need, certainly, is this: how can we help young people into an experience of God's grace, a confidence that they are Christ's? The first reaction may be that a special sermon needs to be preached on the subject or that a lesson in confirmation instruction be devoted to the subject.

Our data show that the problem is more complicated than that. What complicates the issue is that when the gospel is preached, it is often heard in an atmosphere that filters the words. Two out of five persons in A Study of Generations are strongly oriented to the law, and, as such, see structure and form as the essence and reality of the Christian faith. They live a practical atheism, believing that salvation by works is the theology of the church. These law-oriented persons teach this in Sunday school, reflect it in their attitudes, and show it when they emphasize what is Christianity.

How does one communicate a gospel of acceptance, forgiveness, love, trust, in a setting where actions often contradict the words? How can the realities of the faith be experienced non-verbally as well as verbally, where people know forgiveness, love, and trust from members and through these experiences come to understand what God is saying to them?

Many adults who teach youth assume that these young persons have a vital relationship with Christ or assume that if they don't, something is terribly wrong. As a result many youth find it difficult to speak about their feeling of being "out of touch" with God. They are uncomfortable in admitting that they feel they are no longer Christians. I often hear young people complain that no one ever tells them how Christ can become a living reality in their lives. "They only tell us how we are supposed to live." Feeling out of touch with God, they look for someone to tell them how they can know Christ as Savior and as Lord.

NEED FOR RENEWAL

The danger inherent in focusing on youth is to leave the impression that adults "have arrived" spiritually. This is not so. Rebirth and renewal are needed in every age group. It is not true that advancing years and a longer history of church attendance spells deeper faith. As many of the oldest (ages 50-65) believe in salvation by works as do the youngest in our study (ages 15-18). Both groups are alike in their acceptance of a folk religion of doing good. One does not excel the other in perceiving that which distinguishes Christianity from consensus religions.

The oldest (ages 50-65) is as likely as the youngest to support an instrumental view of the church. He is even more likely to de-emphasize the need to spread the gospel. Christianity is seen by as many adults as youth as something we manipulate for our own personal or selfish advantage.

One naturally wonders if the past ten years have brought a change in understanding the Christian faith. Has humanism made its inroads and seriously eroded the perception of adults and youth as to what is distinctively Christian? Some indication for youth is given in the comparison given in the table below. The seven items are simplistic statements of what might be called an American folk religion. They describe a naive religion of salvation by works.

Percent of Lutheran Youth (Age 15-18) Agreeing
with Religion-in-General Items

Item	Percentage Response		
	1959	1962	1970
Salvation depends on being sincere in whatever you believe.	64%		58%
The main emphasis of the Gospel is on God's rules for right livng.	67%		59%
Being tolerant means that one accepts all religions—including Christianity—as equally important before God.	44%		44%
The Bible teaches that God is like a friendly neighbor living upstairs.		59%	40%
God is satisfied if a person lives the best life he can.		48%	70%
A person at birth is neither good nor bad.		40%	50%
Although there are many religions in the world, most of them lead to the same God.		28%	76%
Average (1959 and 1962)	50%		57%

The most striking change in what today's youth believe relates to other religions. Between 1962 and 1970, there was a 48% increase in the number agreeing that "Although there are many religions in the world, most of them lead to the same God." Without question there is a new attitude among young people toward other religions. In addition to this there is a 22% increase in the number who say, "God is satisfied if a person lives the best life he can."

Thinking about youth and their sense of aloneness from God is best done in terms of the larger issue of rebirth and renewal within the church. Our study shows that young people are the most anxious about their faith, the most conscious of a sense of isolation and purposelessness, the most lacking in a perception of grace, and the most receptive to the challenge of the gospel. Youth in the 1970s may take the lead in revitalizing the church by bringing those of all ages to a new awareness of salvation by faith through grace.

What I have said does not mean that because youth feel some apartness from God they are rejecting the historic faith. Less than 4% reject the biblical record, the fact of Christ's life on earth, or the significance of New Testament writings. This mood of alienation does not include a significant number who reject the historical basis for their faith.

This whole discussion on alienation must be understood, also, in the light of adolescent characteristics. It is normal for youth to be clarifying, searching, and trying to establish their identity—including their relationship to the Christian faith. But this does not mean it is a time to be taken for granted by adults and dismissed with the words, "It's just a phase. When they're older they'll settle down and get things sorted out." We are concerned, because many youth leave the church, and reject their faith—permanently.

Chapter 6

How Youth Are Alienated from Church and Adults

Bronfenbrenner, in his book *Two Worlds of Childhood,* says that we are coming to live in a society that is segregated not only by race, but also by age.

Age segregation is also evident in the church. Many organizational activities have become more specialized by age. Except for the Sunday morning worship service it is rare for youth to meet and have fellowship with other adults, and the question might be asked, "How much interchange actually occurs when they do meet?"

ALIENATION FROM THE CHURCH

We found that 43% of the youth (ages 15-23) feel like outsiders in relation to the church family in which they have grown up. Over one-half (52%) are convinced that older people are suspicious of them. They believe that they have no influence on decisions made by the congregation. Even worse, half of the youth say,

"Hardly anyone would miss me if I stopped going." One-half also add, "The church is not doing a good job of involving its youth and of teaching them the Christian life."

This may have been the situation 45 to 50 years ago also. No one knows. But that is not the important issue. The point is that half of the youth feel alienated from the church right now. They feel unwanted, unneeded, and unnoticed.

We analyzed 39 possibilities of disappointment with the church. We found that the strongest predictor of a young person's attitude toward his church is how well he fits in with groups in his congregation. The acceptance he feels is the strongest indicator we could find of how he will evaluate his congregation. If he feels that he fits in poorly and on top of that is uninspired by the Sunday morning services, his attitude toward the church will be a critical one. On the contrary, if he fits in well and is relatively free of pessimism, he will take a positive view. These feelings—fitting into the congregation, being inspired on Sunday morning, and not having a pessimistic attitude—interact more powerfully than the other 36 variables we tested. Feelings are important.

Of the ones who feel they fit in poorly with groups in their congregation, close to three in ten (29%) are at times inspired by the Sunday morning service. Their evaluation of their church is no more critical than the pessimistic-type youth who are part of the "in group" at church.

Serious anti-church feelings are expressed by the 14% who neither fit in nor are ever inspired by the worship service. The strongly negative feelings of this group dramatize the importance of two elements in the life of a congregation: relationships and inspiration. This is seen in the 39% who are most inspired by their

Sunday services and have the most positive feelings toward their congregation. The combination of "fitting in well," not being an overly pessimistic person, and finding some inspiration in the worship services, strongly predicts positive feelings toward a church. Such information indicates what directions and emphases are important in a parish ministry when we are concerned about reaching youth.

Fitting In

Part of the problem of fitting in well with some group relates to how youth feel about themselves. If they have negative attitudes about themselves, others, and life in general, it is difficult to involve them in typical church activities. Unless warmly relating members aggressively reach out to these youth, they remain aloof and seemingly disinterested. Outward impressions, of course, may mask the inner desires of all youth for acceptance into a group of their peers.

How do they feel about themselves? An analysis of the youth with most anti-church feelings shows these characteristics: they tend to feel isolated from any group; more of them are preoccupied with their own advancement, concerned about how they measure up to others, pessimistic about life, rejecting of what the church teaches, and distrustful of adults.

It is well to realize that 15- and 16-year-old youth feel more isolated and out of touch with others than do persons of other ages. This great sensitivity to moods, this feeling of being out of touch with oneself and others, is dramatically illustrated in a single item found in our national surveys of church youth. One out of three (consistently 33%) of youth declare that they sometimes consider suicide.

The implication is, of course, that extra effort needs

to be given to communicating with young people, to showing them that we are interested in them and that we do care. I say extra effort because it is more difficult for youth of this age to believe that anyone is genuinely interested in them. Any efforts made to converse and to communicate do say, of course, "I'm interested in you. I consider you important."

A related reason for disengagement from the life of the church may be both a cause and a reason for some youth being on the outside of their congregation's life. This reason relates to how many of youth's close friends are members of their congregation. To the survey item which asks how many of their five closest friends are members of the congregation they attend, 51% of the 20-29-year-old youth said, "none." This means that the social glue of normal friendships does not draw these youth into their congregation's activity. This is an important loss because youth want to be with their friends. An earlier study (1959) showed that youth organizations encouraged informal friendship groups to be formed within the congregational fellowship. These groups extended the fellowship of the congregation into the week and provided support through the sharing of common beliefs and values. Though this kind of supportive fellowship still continues for many Lutheran youth, it is quite lacking for half the youth.

It has been noted often that youth of today are increasingly religious but quite disenchanted with the institutional church. From our study, we see that this disenchantment with the institutional church, though visible, is less a rejection and more a feeling of detachment from or indifference to the church. One evidence of this detachment is a general lack of participation among those 20-23.

But does this mean that today's youth are not willing to support and help maintain the church in the years ahead? Can we expect declining memberships and budgets because today's youth will no longer be a part of the church that now claims their membership?

Some indications of intended support are given by the items listed below:

	Age Grouping				
	15-19	20-23	24-29	30-49	50-65
I expect that in the future my percentage of giving to the church will be increasing.	63%	63%	67%	56%	40%
I expect that in the future my percentage of giving to the church will be stopping altogether.	5%	5%	2%	1%	1%

For all the talk about youth's reaction to the institution and their strong disenchantment with the church, it is surprising that approximately two out of three (64%) expect that their percentage of giving to the church will increase in the future. Even more surprising is the evidence that no more than 5% expect that their future giving will stop altogether. Apparently there is a basic conviction among the youth that their membership is an important one and that their criticism of the church is primarily a lover's quarrel. If adult prejudices and suspicions of youth are lessened, one can expect a new level of interest and participation among younger members.

Worship Services

Most youth react negatively to the controlled, formal, and unchanging liturgical service. Most youth want free and spontaneous prayers in the service and greater opportunity for a variety of experiences. Three in four (74%) of youth ages 15-23 feel that free and spontaneous prayers are more conducive to worship than those which are written and read. The same high percentage (74%) prefers variety in the morning service to having the same liturgical service Sunday after Sunday. Interestingly, about one out of two adults agree with the youth on both points.

The more formal aspects of a worship service are not important for most persons in our study. Less than a fourth (22%) of either the youngest or the oldest require beauty as an ingredient for a meaningful service. And this percentage drops to 14% for people between ages 19 and 49. A formal, beautiful, but impersonal service is not the preference of most. Even among older adults we find that only one in three (33%) prefers a more formal and liturgical service. For youth ages 15-23 the average is 20%.

In spite of youth's negative attitude toward a formal liturgical service, well over half (56%) like to think that a similar liturgy is employed by other churches throughout the world. The other half, of course, disagree. Though a sense of world-wide community is attractive, what is most important about a worship service is variety, spontaneity, and personal involvement. When these elements are lacking, the youth express their displeasure over what many adults accept with reluctance.

Over a period of years a high school Bible teacher has discussed with her class of high school sophomores the elements they wish were present in a morning worship service. Invariably they say they want an open, informal atmosphere. They want variety, not the same order Sunday after Sunday. The exposition of the Scripture, which traditionally has been in sermon form, should be presented in other ways also, they say. They would like dialog sermons, short drama to illustrate a point, a chance for questions from the audience. They like joyous music (they do not think chorales are happy). They feel worshippers in their church are afraid to smile at each other after they enter the sanctuary, or when they return from taking Holy Communion. They would like prayer involvement by the audience in the worship service, with people sharing prayer requests. They want prayers that speak of everyday life.

One of these classes visited another church one morning, attending an informal service that has been designed especially for youth and young adults. In discussion afterwards, they said they liked that the pastor was dressed casually, and sat on a stool in front of them instead of standing in the pulpit. People from the audience called out songs they would like to sing. Actually, the service was very reverent, but they felt everyone was relaxed and felt free to ask questions. At one point, a young man was asked by the pastor if he would like to share a prayer concern about a boy who had been struggling to break the drug habit.

This same class has discussed how they have difficulty feeling that their pastor has any of the same problems they face. He seems far removed from their world.

By way of understanding why any youth do not like only the sermon approach, it is helpful to remember that they associate it with a teacher's lecture in the classroom, a method which high school youth often consider "boring" and which is being replaced by other educational approaches.

There is a shift in youth's view of God. Unlike older adults, they are conscious of not only God's transcendence but also his immanence. They look for a service that stresses not only his holiness, transcendence, and awesome greatness. They want more than the solemn beauty of a service where architecture, music, and liturgy combine to give one the sense of being in God's presence. Youth want to worship also the God who sits next to them in people and is found in the fellowship of believers.

Youth want to worship a Christ who is not only divine but also human—who is not adverse to rhythm, melody, and ordinary speech. They want a service that inspires and encourages them—that helps them to feel what they are unable to make themselves feel.

Personal observation and the research data lead me to conclude that youth want a service where they *experience* the gospel as well as hear the words. The new mood of today—the expectations which come with a Consciousness III—calls for diversity also in worship approaches. If the item given below is any indication, the resistance will come from a vocal minority only.

Item: Change in Worship:

People react in many different ways when worship services change from what they used to be. Which best describes your feeling?	15-19	Age Groupings			
		20-23	24-29	30-49	50-65
		Percent Agreeing			
a. You are pleased with the changes in worship practices. You favor new ways over old ones because you feel that change means progress.	51%	42%	37%	31%	33%
b. You are unhappy with the changes. You feel that worship services should be kept as they were in the past.	11%	8%	10%	14%	15%
c. You like the old ways of worshiping but don't think you should hang onto them if they don't fit how people feel and think.	37%	48%	53%	54%	49%

ALIENATION FROM ADULTS

The youth showing the most alienation from adults are the 15-16-year-olds. They, more than any other age group, reflect a reaction against adult authority and supervision. Many find high school unbearable and react against anything traditional. Without question their strong anti-adult and anti-authority feelings account in part for the rise of Free Schools and the accent on educational processes where peers teach peers.

Peer-Oriented Youth

A group of youth within the church tend to distrust adults and prefer to take their signals from their own age group. Urie Bronfenbrenner sees peer-oriented youth as more a product of parental disregard than attractiveness of the peer group. They stick to their age mates less by choice than by default.

In our study we did find that most peer-oriented youth see themselves as different from their parents. The majority feel negative about their family and, if given freedom of choice, would have no part in anything run by adults (church, school, political party, family). The ones who are *least* identified with their parents favor or entertain attitudes and practices of the drug culture. Feeling alienated from the adult world, they look for support and a new life style within the counter culture.

When we talk about peer-oriented youth we are talking about one in five ages 15-23. From a depth analysis of our data we find that one or more of the following characteristics are associated with these youth.

A disproportionate number of them are not happy with their family or church; they are the first to accuse adults in the congregation of not caring, and the first to reject the authority of a superior. More of the peer-oriented youth see themselves as different from their parents; more are involved in questionable activities and reflect an attraction to a life of detachment from the world's demands. A larger number of these youth reject transcendental values, do not admit to a personal caring God, and commonly feel isolated and under pressure. They want their pastor to become involved in public demonstrations and civil disobedience; they advocate service to people without a proclamation of the gospel, and believe that issues of social justice and reform are essentially power struggles. They hold doubts or negative attitudes about their own faith, view death as unknowable or as the end of life, are pessimistic about others, and are least convinced of a Christian hope.

Though these characteristics tend to be found among peer-oriented youth, it does not mean that all these youth believe, think, or act these ways. It only means that these strongly alienated youth often express themselves in these ways. One undoubtedly will find some peer-oriented youth who contrast in some ways with the descriptions given here.

To illustrate, most peer-oriented youth distrust adults, but some do not. This is seen in their answers to the following items. Although 19% are alienated from adults, fewer than that say they distrust adults.

	Age Groupings	
	15-19	20-23
My first reaction to adults is to suspect their motives. I don't trust them.	11%	6%
Contrary to what is being said, I trust many adults over 30 years of age.	16%	15%
The only ones I really trust are other people about my age.	6%	2%

This illustration points out why generalizations about youth must be lightly held and not used to classify or pigeonhole youth. We can use information on subgroups in determining a strategy for a youth ministry but not to prejudge individuals. We can accent activities which enhance a trust relationship without approaching youth with the assumption they distrust adults. From what we know of peer-oriented youth, a congregation is well advised to equip its older youth for reaching out to them.

Inasmuch as youth of ages 15-23 see the local congregation as run by adults, their attitude toward adults is important. If it is anti-adult, it is likely that they are also anti-church in their feelings. This fact is abundantly clear in the data.

We found that the stronger youth's feelings of disappointment in their church, the stronger their distrust of adults. Also, the youth least able to trust "anyone over 30" are not the college age youth (whom many adults fear will topple institutions as they get older). Rather they are the youngest of the youth age. There is no evidence of a tidal wave of distrust among youth ages 21-23 that will result in a mass exodus of institutional support. Rather, the evidence is that the attitude associated with the college age youth in the late 1960s has slipped down into the high school or late teen period. It is the youth still at home who voice the most distrust of adults and who respond most eagerly to their peer group. Roughly one in five (19%) are strongly anti-church and anti-adult. Most of these youth (15% of all Lutheran youth) are much involved in questionable personal practices. They are the youth least able or least willing to delay personal gratification.

A dramatic illustration of how alienation from church and adults interrelate is seen also on the positive side. Those expressing *least* anti-adult feelings are the 23% of Lutheran youth who are *least* disappointed with their church.

Establishing Communication

How does a parent meet this problem when he finds it in his home? Many fathers come home tired from work and are not ready to give themselves to the family. One study shows that when children are in their teen years, communication between husband and wife is at the lowest level (Blood and Wolfe, 1960). Yet this is a time when the lines should be most open. This is a time when husband and wife need to think through how to stay in touch with each other and with their teenage youth. One must decide how to react to the unreasonableness within oneself and the peer-oriented youth without making the problem a greater one.

We have found that a Parent Effectiveness Training program is a welcomed addition in the life of many parents. This program helps parents identify the problems that belong to them, the problems that belong to the child, and the problems which belong to both of them. The program teaches parents how to listen actively, how to become attuned to feelings as well as words (Gordon, 1971). Parents also learn to communicate their own feelings when they are hurting or distressed. Further, they learn and practice skills of problem solving when they face a conflict situation with one or more family members.

The Division of Youth Activity of The American Lutheran Church has developed a similar program for parents, called P.A.C.T. (Parent/Adult Covenant Theatre). This program offers a blend of an invitation to soul-searching in the area of parent-child relationships, and the introduction to some new communications skills. It provides a "covenant" community where parents can support each other in their mutual covenant with God and their children. It involves parents in a "theatre" of involvement. Parents play roles and rehearse for the drama of parent-child life together at home. Youth are involved in parts of the program, along with adults.

Self-Destructive Activities

Especially disturbing to parents and youth leaders, of course, is the proneness of peer-oriented youth to become involved in immoral and self-destructive activities. Premarital sex, drug abuse, and drinking are highly associated with these youth (see *A Study of Generations,* for further discussion).

We have always known that problems of ethical behavior are common to junior high, high school, and college youth. Traditionally, we have associated impulse with youth and restraint with adults. Lest this distinction be exaggerated, let me quickly add that the willingness or ability to delay gratification is not a problem restricted to youth. Approximately the same number of adults in A Study of Generations answered as did the youth on two items relating to gratification: 35% agreed that they had no moral reason for delaying pleasure, 55% said that they would enjoy now rather than wait for whatever seemed pleasurable.

CONCLUSION

In challenging the negative images adults hold of youth, we cannot say that "all is well." On the contrary, we must acknowledge what youth of high school and college age have reported about themselves, and how they feel about their church, and God. A large proportion feel outside the faith, unwanted by the adult congregation, and in some cases, like rebellious captives within the institution. Symptomatic expression of their apartness is seen in life styles that often lead to self-destructive behavior.

These youth need to rediscover who they are—to feel that they are indeed children of God and a part of his eternal family. They need also to find a sense of mission that can give them a reason for living. They need to become committed to a cause and a Person who will lead them to significance and meaning.

The last thing they need are walls of condemnation that serve only to increase their aloneness. Adults need the mind of Christ who can look at each one of us and say we are children of God. Effective youth work begins in the hearts and minds of the adult congregation.

*The biblical story of the ninety and nine is
a story of concern for the lost. This section is
concerned with how we can bring youth back
"in touch" with God and their church. How
do we best help youth find their identity in
Christ?*

PART THREE

Finding and Being Found

Introduction

The purpose of this section is to think together on
how youth can be helped to find their identity as children of God. Some, caught in the problems of an
identity diffusion, do not know who they are, and this
makes them feel anxious and uncertain. Others choose
a negative identity and adopt a pattern of living, believing, and valuing the opposite of what they idealize.
Still others know who they are and need help only
in identity formation.

Identity formation is nothing more than the process
of becoming what we are. When we are married we
are given a new role, yet we are a lifetime in becoming
married. When a child is baptized in the Christian
faith, he is given a new identity, yet he spends a lifetime becoming a Christian and coming to know who
he is. Adults have a responsibility in helping youth
to know who they are in Christ.

Chapter 7

The Mutuality Found in a Community of Faith

What do I mean by the word mutuality? An attitude of mutuality includes an openness to change, a willingness to share oneself with another. Mutuality implies a growing together with another person or group of persons. When an adult is working with a youth, mutuality is exemplified by a relationship of co-seeking, co-helping, and co-working. The adult in this case views the youth as a whole being whose personhood he needs. Mutuality builds on the conviction that many of the problems we face cannot be solved in isolation. It is a recognition that one of us cannot "go it alone," that we deeply and truly need each other.

Mutuality is fostered by the attitude that "no one has arrived," that everyone, regardless of age or experience, is daily in need of judgment and God's forgiveness.

It is in the setting of a family, or another kind of

accepting group, that a person first experiences mutuality and the reality of being important to others. The interaction and sense of community that typifies a family best illustrates the concept of mutuality. Family is crucial to identity formation.

NEEDED: A SENSE OF FAMILY

I am referring primarily to the *experiences* which give a person a sense of being a part of a family. In a family setting youth have the experience of communicating in depth, meeting the judgment and acceptance of a respected group, coming to understand their own experiences by sharing them within that group. Family members are those with whom a youth can identify, whose beliefs and values are ones he can make his own. For in claiming and coming to know a people, a history, a tradition, and a style of life with which he can identify, a person comes to know himself.

I stress the concept of family because many studies of alienated youth show that alienated youth have alienating parents. In many cases these adults want to be good parents, but their style of interaction is such that they create barriers between themselves and their children. Some, of course, alienate through indifference, absence, or dissension in the home. The closest parent-child relationships develop where *both* see the need for personal reevaluation and growth.

This means that a youth ministry does not consist only in what is done for youth. It means also work with adults to help them face feelings and attitudes that build barriers between themselves and young people. Inextricably linked, of course, with an openness to man is openness to God. A first essential in a youth ministry is a cadre of adults who are open enough in their relationships to God and man to share themselves and their faith with another person.

This concept of mutuality will be resisted by many in a congregation because the idea stands in opposition to the rigidity, perfectionism, and instrumentalism that characterize almost half the adult congregation. As many resist change as welcome it; about two in five are religious absolutists who do not want any tampering with the present program. But an accent on mutual interaction can open doors for needed changes.

Adults who work with youth in a church setting must give increasing significance to the "non-kindred family," the family that is made up of friends. Some young people do not have a kindred family, and so a church fellowship must provide both the experience of communicating in depth, and the people with whom they can identify. The church of Jesus Christ does have a history, a tradition, a people, and a style of life that can become the one "family" which some youth know.

Communes or communal living offer a way for some to recover a sense of family or community. One example is the Camden Youth Ministry which Larry Nelson helped establish under the Board of American Missions of the Lutheran Church in America. Seventeen youth are trying to form a Christian community through communal living with Pastor Bob. Together they are trying to develop a pattern that will fit everyone who "wants in."

A family setting and approach has a unique contribution to make to a program of Christian education. This is being recognized and applied in many places. Note for instance what one of my reviewers penned on the side of her manuscript: "We have started a family Sunday school class at home with three families

76

because our children object to the 'school' approach on Sunday morning. We have a class of 18 ranging in age from 4 to 45."

We have fascinating research data on religious development through families reported in *Research in Religious Development*. I say fascinating because the two elements which emerge as the most powerful factors in religious development are family congeniality and parental religious values.

Congeniality: what does that have to do with religious training? When a home is characterized by an atmosphere of congeniality, then parental values are effectively communicated because the young people identify with their parents. This research finding simply reinforces the obvious fact that non-verbal factors of living together in a community of freedom and joy are important educational tools.

Parental religious values, too, are communicated naturally. If the parents are committed to a faith, and the relationship is a congenial one, then the young person is most likely to share his parents' faith For such youth outside influences like a parochial school education are minor, except to reinforce what the home has already established.

An important consideration in any approach to youth work is the climate and vitality of the community or group which communicates the faith. The evidence seems clear that as important as what is taught formally is the relationship established by the people who are doing the teaching. Classes and youth meetings must engender a sense of family so that the truths which are being taught can be experienced in the setting of a family. Theologizing can then become the rational effort to understand the love and acceptance that has been experienced.

77

NEEDED: ADULTS OF WARMTH

Keniston, in his classic study of alienation, shows that the heart of alienation is distrust, and our study verifies that conclusion.

Distrust is a major barrier to overcome. Adults who work with "unattached" youth find that three to seven months are needed to establish rapport and gain acceptance with them. Alienated youth have learned *not* to open their lives to anyone lest they be exploited. They have learned *not* to be intimate.

For this reason a youth ministry must be carried out in a setting that engenders a sense of trust, openness, and acceptance. And who establishes this climate? People who have found an identity in life and are willing to share themselves with others. Alienated youth need not so much expertise as the human qualities of warmth, empathy, and genuineness. Research has shown that we need adults who can "ride loose in the saddle" without losing their concern for youth.

Recent studies show the contribution of these human qualities and what can be accomplished by non-experts.

A quiet revolution in psychology began in 1952 when Eysenck, an English psychologist, reported on his reviews of the outcomes of psychotherapy. He concluded that people might just as well not bother with psychotherapy—sugar pills are just as effective and much cheaper.

His gadfly statements introduced a frantic note into the profession and soon the psychological journals were carrying articles pro and con. Twelve years later a review of the research studies came up with essentially the same conclusion as Eysenck's.

But a puzzle remained. Through therapeutic counseling, some people were actually finding a sense of personal reality and were giving evidence of having been helped. What factors could account for their being helped? More studies were conducted, and these findings began to surface.

It is not technique, but the human qualities of *warmth, empathy,* and *genuineness* that account for effective therapy.

What if these qualities are missing in the therapist?

Truax, at the University of Wisconsin, showed that when several highly trained therapists lacked these qualities, the condition of their extremely alienated patients deteriorated. But when other therapists, also highly trained, ranked well in the qualities of warmth, empathy, and genuineness, their counselees made notable advances.

The evidence is quite clear: the important factor in helping another person to a sense of trust and an identity is not having a technique or being an expert. Rather, it is the factor of an empathetic and warm relationship. It does not matter so much what is discussed, as that the interchange establishes a relationship.

If the important essentials in helping youth to personal significance are empathy, warmth, and genuineness, then untrained youth and adults can be effective. Carefully selected lay people are well able to relate to alienated persons with positive outcomes. That means that ordinary people in a congregation can serve as substitute parents, providing they are free to open their lives to others.

The revolution I described in the mental health professions has another profound implication for youth work.

Generally, in youth work churches and schools have followed the medical model; that is, a person of superior knowledge examines someone who needs help. Once the doctor makes a diagnosis, he gives a prescription and expects that it will be carried out.

But this model is now up for question, in youth work as well as therapy. A more appropriate approach for adults who work with youth is the model of mutual exchange. Here it is not the stronger helping the weaker, but two people fulfilling their incompleteness in each other. Here the adult is not concerned with the deep psychological underground world of the youth. Rather, his concern is with communication that flows two ways. Each person, youth and adult, shares his hopes and fears, insights and perplexities, convictions and doubts. The person usually called the "teacher" believes he can learn from the person usually called the "learner."

This approach makes sense to me as a Christian. For I believe that the Shepherd himself is present during my conversations with a youth. Regardless of the topic, the two of us share not only ourselves, but also share him.

In it all, the Word of God is trying to communicate the truth of forgiveness to both youth and adult. The purpose, then, is to realize anew the truth implied in the question, "Do you know that your sins are forgiven in Jesus Christ?"

It is this message that makes the relationships unique. Not that adults manipulate their conversations to speak about forgiveness. Rather, forgiveness is reflected in the sense of hopefulness possessed by an adult who works with youth. And at appropriate times it is expressed also in words.

NEEDED: A COMMUNITY OF FAITH

If we assume that a youth ministry should seek a climate of trust through substitute parents and an atmosphere of openness through mutual exchange, then we are talking about qualities that characterize also a community of faith. Here I refer both to the congregational community and the youth community.

Congregational Community

We can underestimate the influence and impact of the interlocking relationships found in some congregations. Though the interchange is infrequent and often quite unnoticed, there is a sustaining fellowship of friendship and love that nourishes the lives of many people. I have always acknowledged the doctrine of the church, to be sure, and given lip service to what it is. But I was slow to realize that a community of faith, though its ties may be slender and loosely woven, does generate a climate of concern and interest. And this atmosphere of caring for one another makes a difference in the lives of all who breathe its life-giving air.

This is strikingly evidenced in some of our studies. We made one analysis to determine differences among youth when divided according to the type and extent of their congregation's youth activities. We wanted to know whether real differences in the youth themselves would show on the basis of types of youth programs. Surprisingly, no differences appeared.

But, when we divided the youth on the basis of adults' concern and sensitivity for youth, we found significant differences between the youth. In congregations where lay adults expressed most concern for youth, we found the youth in greatest "health." And the opposite was also true. Where the adults showed least sensitivity and concern, irrespective of the formal youth program, we found the youth to be in greatest trouble.

One of the strengths of a congregation is its inter-generational life style. Rather than encourage age separation in the general routine of church activities, more should be done to bring youth and adults together in cooperative activities. When there is personal and warm interaction, adults can serve as models for the youth and youth can serve as encouragers to the adults. Tension will surface at times, but this allows for healthy identification. As youth and adults come to know one another as persons of concern and dedication, their negative stereotypes of each other lose their power.

As we grow older we are less open to change. We have a greater need for unchanging structures. We need a more dogmatic position in religious matters. We have a greater desire to be with people who are like us, and shy away from people who are quite different. We have a greater tendency to exaggerate the importance of our church. We depend more on following organizational procedures. Because we tend to change in ways that make us more rigid, we need to listen to youth who can help us remain flexible, open, and youthful in spirit. They constantly alert us to ways in which a "rigor mortis of spirit" can set in and unconsciously make us examples of the law rather than living gospels. Youth and adults need each other to know a sense of community and a sense of mission.

Youth Community

A second necessary community of faith is one formed by youth themselves. This experience is vital because it provides a different and necessary framework within which youth can find themselves. Youth need a smaller group where members find the freedom to admit their doubts, sins, weaknesses, and ignorance. Members of such a group learn to listen to one another and, in doing so, to hear God speak. As they try to help one another crystallize in words the truths they experience, they learn a living theology.

For youth whose homes are filled with a mood of despair, this kind of non-kindred family fellowship can be inspirational therapy. Of course, these small group experiences do not just happen. Surrogate parents are required. Such leaders help establish a model of mutual exchange by themselves entering into conversations as ones who believe they are helped in helping, and are taught in teaching. They need to be adults who teach as one who is learning, with and alongside the young people.

In this approach youth and adults have a mutual ministry to each other. They share themselves, their convictions, their faith with each other. Each generation learns to respond to the mood of the other. Youth work using this model of mutuality is, in effect, a call to greater fulfillment. As youth open their lives to each other and come to realize that they are part of the community of faith, they establish a new basis for identity—the family of God. This family has ideals they can make their own.

NEEDED: ONE-TO-ONE RELATIONSHIPS

When a young person becomes the focus of a conversation with a concerned adult, the young person experiences the personal warmth, empathy, and concern of the listening adult. This experience in mutuality is in itself an important outcome of the encounter. The process of self-disclosure often leads the youth to a personal relationship with God, or a decreased sense of alienation, or release from certain inner conflicts. The self-disclosure that results from one-to-one conversations is a necessary, though insufficient, condition for finding one's identity.

I stress this one-to-one ministry because it represents a viable approach to the lonely and alienated in a congregation and can be carried out especially by older youth. Some young adults in their late teens or early twenties are able to reach out with a helping relationship to peer-oriented youth who shun the organized youth activities of a church. Their ministry, though not one of numbers, is of strategic importance. They may be the church's last contact with youth who are drifting out of fellowship with God and a community of faith.

At our Youth Research Center in Minneapolis we have tested three approaches in training youth to reach out to lonely and alienated youth (in our Project YOUTH). As a result of this program, a total of 493 friendships were formed by youth in the Project with young people living on the edge of life. We have had many experiences that illustrate the potential for youth to reach out to youth. For example, a high school girl asked a staff member of our Center, "What's Project YOUTH all about?" When asked why she came to ask, she replied in effect, "Today I watched in amazement as a very popular guy in our school (he's in Project YOUTH) delayed leading a play rehearsal because he saw my very troubled girl friend hurting and came over to talk to her. She was so down she hadn't talked all day in or out of class. Nobody had been able to reach her—me included. In ten minutes he had her talking, caring about life again. She left as a different person. If that's what Project YOUTH is all about, being able to do that for people, I want in!"

How does one converse with youth? Let me mention

three guidelines that help establish a congenial climate and the experience of mutuality.

1. *Carry on conversations as one person trying to understand the other.* Everyone knows we are supposed to listen to others. But interestingly, we adults are not talking with youth long before we begin functioning as a doctor, asking one question after another. Instead of trying to understand what a young person is saying, we are trying to figure out what question to ask next. When we do this we are no longer listening.

Active listening is a posture we take when we are truly interested and concerned about someone. It is a complementary relationship that tends to form friendships. This kind of one-to-one relationship is an essential ingredient in the life of the church because it involves the giving of oneself. This empathetic listening with a warm and positive regard means much to people of any age. I say this because we will never fully learn that loneliness is a fact of life, and that longing is an attribute of man. This is especially true for the youth age. This is why some young people find it a unique experience to converse with someone who responds to them in the same mood as they are feeling.

We listen not only to the voice of the young person in order to resonate with him. We also listen for the voice of God to tell us what we can say—to know the fitting word. Here we who live by his promise believe that we are not left to our own resources.

2. *Seek to awaken a sense of hope.* During the times we talk with a young person we hear him share painful memories, nagging fears, or deep-felt inadequacies. It would not be honest of us to gloss over these feelings and try to reassure the person that these are not as bad as they seem.

What we can do is listen out of the conviction that there is hope for everyone, regardless of his situation. A conviction such as this will be reflected in our responses and in our very demeanor. Non-verbally, we will convey the message of good news also for this person. His life can be significant. God, who has changed people in the past, can change them today. The promises that God has given to men in the past, he continues to give today. And every promise speaks of possibilities.

Most young people have really not heard this message for themselves. In general, they view forgiveness as a blotter for past misdeeds; they regard salvation as primarily a passport to heaven. Few know that God can bring power to their lives now, and that he enters not to solve problems but to transform lives. It is of this hope that we must speak.

I've been talking about our becoming involved in an encounter, an interaction between three people where God is the third person. In these conversations, his hand can reach over our shoulders to touch the young life. In doing so, God communicates something far beyond the words that we say. Lest I minimize verbal message, let me say that there will come times when the young person asks the kind of question that requires answering with the story of what God has done and can do.

3. *Participate in life.* In the past we have seen counseling (whether adult with youth or youth with youth) as focusing on the individual and his relationship to himself, people, or God. Now we are coming to see how one's personal life is entangled with broader issues. Personal problems cannot be separated from family, institutional, and national problems. Therefore, mutuality also means that we participate with another

person or a group in acting, in doing something to change vexing or intolerable situations. This leads us to the concept of mission as part of mutuality. In other words, mutuality is both *being* and *doing*.

CONCLUSION

Both youth and adults need and want the mutuality and warmth found in an accepting person. This sense of mutuality profoundly influences what any person believes about himself, his world, and his God.

A youth ministry needs to develop a sense of family, to seek out adults of personal warmth and concern, to establish a feeling of community, and to encourage conversations between youth and adults. These are important elements in breaking through the barrier of distrust and helping youth into a sense of identity. It is the antidote for youth reared in homes where parents have not been able to establish a sense of family. It provides the setting in which youth and adults together can come to a sense of their impor-tance and worth in Jesus Christ and their identity in the family of God.

Chapter 8

The Sense of Commitment Found in Mission

The second major imperative in youth work is to help youth into a feeling of mission, of being sent— of being sent for a purpose and a task. It is to know the sense of purposefulness that grips the person who has responded to God's love.

I was struck by the clarity with which these two polarities—mutuality and mission—emerged in A Study of Generations as essential elements in a life of faith. When these two are missing in the life of a young person, he probably feels alienated from God. We discovered through a depth analysis that the two most powerful predictors of a life alienated from God are the opposites of mutuality and mission. They are feelings of isolation and feelings of purposelessness.

ADULTS AND MAINTENANCE GOALS

A major problem in congregations is the lack among adults of a strong sense of "being sent" for a purpose or a task. Most adults are not aware of this lack, however. Two-thirds of the laity over 40 years of age think that members in their congregation know the purpose of the congregation. But the majority of the clergy and youth disagree with them. The clergy and youth feel that "maintenance goals" which center in budget, membership, and buildings take priority. The contentedness of older adults with the status quo is seen in the fact that half (47%) say without qualification that they are happy with their church. No more than 19% of the clergy and 21% of the youth give that statement.

More serious, even, than this smugness is the distorted view of mission held by two out of five, both youth and adults. For them, Christianity is primarily a tool for gaining personal goals, a self-oriented utilitarianism. Coupled with this view of Christianity is a denial of the need to share the gospel.

Undermining any sense of mission is a simplistic belief system that has two basic features: it accepts all religions as equal to Christianity, and it assents to a work righteousness. Though this misbelief or heresy finds acceptance among all ages, the youngest (15-18) and the oldest (50-65) are the most prone to believe this way. Specifically, three out of five accept a religion of good works as defining their idea of Christianity. This notable evidence of an inadequate base for mission dramatizes the importance of why "getting one's own head on straight" is a prerequisite of mission.

RADICALS VS. REVOLUTIONARIES

Those concerned about social action are propelled by two different orientations—a power orientation and a gospel orientation. This says much about the way in which mission and mutuality depend on each other.

Youth and adults who have not dealt with issues within themselves, though socially concerned and involved, can be a "sounding brass."

One or more of the following characterize those who are power-oriented. Though they declare a desire to eliminate justice, inequality, and cruelty, and though they want their church to become involved in social issues, they are actually as rigid and bigoted as the people they criticize. A disproportionate number are pessimistic about the world and convinced that any means to accomplish their crusade is justifiable. Theirs is a power orientation to social action. They could be called "radicals" as distinguished from "revolutionaries"—of which Christ was one. Youth and adults with this power orientation are less likely to profess a strong faith. Theologically they identify with a law orientation. They believe in a salvation by works and favor service without proclamation. They do not consider the Good News important. The phony liberal and the reactionary crusader are both in this group.

Mission can be self-serving when religion is considered something one *uses* for personal purposes.

A second and larger group of social action minded Lutherans are gospel-oriented. They see God as a personal caring God, have an attitude of openness to others, and are positively oriented to themselves and life. This group considers not only the *ends* of social justice important but also the *means* used to achieve the ends. As revolutionaries seeking to bring about change they take seriously the servant path that Christ followed.

AVAILABLE: A NEW WILLINGNESS TO SERVE

A person working with high school youth is often faced with two sharp contradictions. On the one hand, it seems that their chief concern is themselves—getting dates, making money, finding friends, having adventurous experiences, being attractive to others. Even their protests and demands for change in the school system are often for their own advantage.

Survey findings verify this. Youth is definitely a time of preoccupation with establishing one's place in the sun (and no doubt must be). The peak interest in self-development values (for example, high priority given to pleasure, physical appearance, recognizing personal power) occurs for the 15 and 16 year olds. This strong self-interest, however, drops off sharply for 19 year olds and levels off for people 24 years and above. A youth leader or parent can, then, expect young people in their mid-teens to be heavily preoccupied with their own advancement and self-development.

But here comes the contradiction. Along with this strong self-interest, there is today among the majority of youth an undeniable search for significance and meaning. This search is especially evident among young adults. This is documented in a Yankelovitch study of a cross-section of American students. College youth responded this way: 79% said that they believe commitment to a meaningful career is a very important part of a person's life; 76% would welcome less emphasis on money; 70% said the top influence in their career choice is the chance to make a contribution. Their answers show that the mood of students today is a desire to be a part of something significant. For them, mission is important.

In our surveys of 1959 and 1962 I found little concern among high school youth over national or world issues. But today this has changed. Worries over war, pollution, disorder, racism, social justice, and poverty are widespread concerns. Youth are deeply offended by prejudice and the social distance that separates church members from people of contrasting life styles. They are troubled by the injustice and suffering that dogs the steps of so many people. Thousands in one city alone will walk 20-30 miles as a demonstration of concern and earn money for underprivileged in various parts of the world. We have discovered that the more concerned youth are, the more they are oriented to change. They want social action now.

But here comes the frustration. When it comes to actual service, action lags behind rhetoric. There is a contrast for most youth between what they say should be done and what they do themselves. This is true for youth up to the age of 23. This mismatch of rhetoric and action is seen also among young people in colleges and universities who will mass in great demonstrations of protest but fail to show up for the ongoing activities of giving help over a sustained period of time. Heath questions the depth of this generation's commitment in his book, *Humanizing Schools*. He summarizes studies since 1968 showing that not more than two to ten percent of the students on any campus have participated in any social or protest activity. More frequently the issues that galvanize students into action are self-serving ones dealing with dress and societal rules.

How do we account for the contrast between rhetoric and action? Why is it that youth are the least involved of all ages up to 65 in helping activities, in showing neighborliness, in helping friends who are caught in crisis situations, and in political and community activities?

One obvious answer is that the natural self-development drive during this period of life militates against following through on good intentions which involve self-denial.

Feuer, in *Conflict of Generations,* has another explanation. He notes that youth have risen at different times in history as society's voice of conscience to protest adult indifference to social need. It is his observation, however, that these mission-oriented efforts are short-lived and that youth out of discouragement soon give up their idealistic efforts.

I see today's situation as different because the mission concern—the sense of urgency to act—is not limited to the youth population. The majority of adults share youth's feelings that the church must be sensitive to people who are hurting. There is a discernible shift in the concept of ministry and mission. A majority of adults are ready to join the youth.

A shift in attitude is also discerned among leaders in big business. Herbert Bissell, a former corporate vice-president for Honeywell Inc., takes note of this in his book, *Big Business—Your Life*. He insists that there is a greater sense of community responsibility among business leaders and a greater willingness to pay their "social rent," than there had been in the past.

I believe the 1970s will see an increasing number of youth who match rhetoric with action. I believe youth's feeling for people is more than a faddish concern. It is part of the new mood in church and society. There is an increasing concern for the welfare of individuals and a resurgence of interest in a biblically-oriented Christianity. For that reason I take seriously the statements of one out of three youth who, though not involved in service activities of their church or community, declare a willingness to participate if asked.

It's hard to chart trends, but the evidence points to a readiness for mission that may be different from past decades. Young people around the country are responding in a new way to opportunities for ministering to human need.

To illustrate, a Youth Tutoring program which developed in 1967 is now a national program with nearly 400 cities participating. Most of the tutors of high school or junior high school age are in academic difficulty themselves. They teach elementary school children on a one-to-one basis (Resources for Youth, 1971).

Since 1969, hundreds of youth-oriented telephone emergency services and walk-in services have surfaced around the country. Related services such as free clinics, information and referral centers, drug help, and suicide centers have blossomed also. By January, 1972, a National Directory of Hotlines, Switchboard, and Related Services listed approximately 500 centers, most of which are staffed by volunteers who are youth or young adults.

Similarly, mission-oriented activities are becoming part of the life of congregations and colleges. Concordia College (River Forest, Illinois) has 365 students involved in some type of tutoring or service activity.

Congregations in all parts of the country are reporting innovative activities that meet some community or personal need.

AVAILABLE: SERVICE THROUGH THE CHURCH

Many persons look into the future and wonder whether or not today's youth will live out their concerns within existing institutions. Some assume that the strong anti-institutional feelings of the late 1960s will roll like a tidal wave into the adult years. This does not seem to be happening.

Recent polls show a revival of interest in biblically-oriented evangelical Christianity, a resurgence that is being compared with the rise of youthful radicalism in the '60s. On many college campuses, and certainly the church-related campuses, they have become the single most visible force on campus. Reasons for the wide appeal of this new movement include:

1. Disillusionment with the established church, with the quality of American life, and with the fads of youth countercultures.

2. A hunger for personal meaning and significance.

3. An attraction to the simplicity, authoritativeness, and demands of an evangelical Christianity.

Surveys show that 1970 (the year we collected our data) was a high point in radical feelings. Students the next year were far less critical of the major institutions than they were in 1970. Two out of three students in 1970 thought student radicalism would continue to grow, but in 1971, the number who thought this had dropped to one in three. The majority of students said their preferred method of bringing about change was to work within the system (65%) or to do what one could do in his own community (78%).

In our study we found similar support for the institutional church. The number unwilling to serve within the church was not large. No more than three in ten (about 30%) on the average said they would refuse to serve as an officer in the church, to teach Sunday school or Bible class, to attend a church convention as a delegate or to work for the youth of the church. The responses of people 30-49 years old were the same, so we can conclude that youth are as willing to serve as are adults of middle age.

More significant is the percentage of youth who declare an eagerness to serve. (The items allow respondents to report what they have done willingly, or would do gladly if asked.) It is impressive that at least three in five (60% or more) of the youth affirm their support of the church by what they say they would be willing to do. The response of youth compares favorably with that of adults in the two older age groupings. In other words, there is no evidence from the data that today's youth will give less support to the institutional church than older adults will give.

It is significant that the majority of youth (63%) are convinced that the message of the church is an antidote for the malady of selfishness and is absolutely needed in today's world. More of the adults (76%) view the church in this hopeful way. Both groups, however, show general agreement (7 in 10) that preaching the gospel and working toward improving the material well-being of people are both equally important. The problem for more of the youth is that they simply feel these two emphases are out of balance. It is their conviction that far too little has been done in becoming involved in social issues. This opinion is held by more than half (55%) of the youth. It is a smaller group of youth and adults who think that "too much" has been done. Their proportions range from one in five youth (22%) to one in three (35%) adults.

Social action in relation to sharing the gospel in word is like mutuality in relation to mission. Both are essential to each other. It is significant that the majority of young people agree that God's words of forgiveness must be at the heart of mission activity. In our study 82% of the youth affirm that the primary task of the church is to preach the gospel. They recognize the need for times of clarifying, verbalizing, and sharing their faith with others. This they can do with a persuasiveness that often eludes adults.

NEEDED: MODELS OF CARING

Our incompleteness as a church has been in the realm of *mission*. Our approach to youth of the church has been a shelter model of feeding and keeping. We have done little to *equip* and *send* our youth into areas of need. The same can be said with respect to adults. We need to develop ways and means of doing this. One of the best ways is to provide examples.

Young people need a model—someone whose life inspires commitment, someone who is not teaching words, but incarnating within his own life a deep feeling for the hungry and maligned, the dispossessed, the outcast. In short, they need someone who embodies in himself the spirit of Christ. A primary resource for such models may be young adults.

Adults can model a spirit of service and an attitude toward others that the young people can't help but pick up. It is another form of communication. It is what happens in a family that knows a congenial atmosphere of trust and acceptance. The children tend to adopt the values and beliefs of their parents.

This modeling is especially potent when the person who is the model is liked and admired, when he takes a special interest in people around him, when he serves in a major role of support and control (such as a parent, teacher, youth director), and when his life is one with which others can identify. I am convinced that a youth leader makes as great an impact by his modeling as he does by the program he brings into being.

Interaction of age, of course, must go beyond a few select leaders. It ought to include the entire congregation. But here we face one of the invisible barriers to mission within a congregation. Though adults want young people to be occupied with youth activities—a kind of make-believe church—they may not want to welcome them as full partners in the task of carrying out the church's mission. This age segregation with respect to the serious business of the church leaves both young and old poorer in spirit and resources.

Accepting children and youth as partners in the church's mission does have its irritations and its tensions for both generations. But these can become occasions for learning from one another—the teachable moments.

I am convinced that the Christian faith and a sense of commitment become most alive in a setting of conflict. I am impressed by the fact that youth with the clearest sense of goal often come out of homes and communities where there is great opposition. Often the youth who have thought through what they believe and are best able to speak with conviction and clarity are those who have been challenged to give some answers. The youth who have adopted an ethic of responsibility are the ones who have been exposed to temptation and become convinced that God's law has been given to them primarily out of love. They have experienced in school that a class comes alive when someone opposes their faith and wants to know why they believe as they do.

Here I am speaking of controversy not as a game of intellectual ping-pong among a group of intellectual dilettantes, but the serious grappling with issues that involve the happiness and welfare of many. I am speaking here of issues which touch the heart, the feelings, the very core of one's life and which can lead to conviction and commitment.

NEEDED: LIVES OF COMMITMENT

Life demands commitment. Not only the commitment of accepting responsibilities but the central commitment of obedience to a transcendent God. It is out of this basic commitment that a sense of mission flows.

In the garden of Gethsemane we see a union of commitment with honesty. Christ made it plain that if he did as his feelings wanted, he would not go to the cross. Hence, he accepted this mission in a full awareness of his resistance and not his repression. He did not block out one in favor of the other, but kept both the "is" and the "should be" in dialog.

In the same way, youth need the honest expression of feelings that is found in the experiences of mutuality. But they need also the challenge of a "should be," God's call to every man. Here is a striking example of how this can be incorporated in the life of a congregation:

Discovering the Mission. St. Peter's Lutheran Church, located in the South Bronx, New York City, is in a community overwhelmed with urban problems. Some of the most serious are: *housing* —high density apartments, approximately 80% of which range from deteriorated to dilapidated; *health*—drug abuse, veneral disease, anemia, lead poisoning, infant mortality and TB at the highest rates in the city; *education*—many children graduate from elementary school without being able to read or write; *spirit*—the community is suffering and dying and fighting for survival.

Responding with Commitment. St. Peter's has become known through the years as a church that cares about the needs of the community and acts to bring hope to the people who live there. It operates a parochial school which children and parents beg to enter because it affords a much greater opportunity for learning. With other community groups and churches, it is part of a housing association sponsoring 200 new housing units and is working for the redevelopment of the block in which the church is located.

In coalition with 10 South Bronx churches from many denominations, St. Peter's has helped to establish a house for ex-drug addicts. It is a 24-hour residential community of males living together in a therapeutic setting. Called "Wayout," the residence is a place where the men learn to share secrets with God and each other, where no physical violence is permitted at any time and where trust and love enable persons to change former destructive attitudes and behavior.

Each act of service is done in the context of worship—in an effort to make what we do and say on Sunday morning a reality during the week. In like fashion what we do during the week becomes integrated into the worship on Sunday: ecumenical services in abundance to celebrate and suffer together in crises—be they housing, drug abuse, education—but always affirming oneness in Jesus Christ. *(Grass Roots, Report #1)*

HOW MUTUALITY AND MISSION ARE RELATED

I have presented an approach to youth work that centers in two polarities—mutuality and mission. These two emphases complement each other in the same way that freedom complements responsibility, free expression complements self-denial, and structure complements creativity. Sara Little comes to a similar conclusion in her book, *Youth, World, and Church,* in which she gives helpful guidelines and a theological rationale for mission and nurture.

Although I have used separate chapters to discuss mutuality and mission, you should not view them as separate facets of a youth ministry, but rather as interrelated. Each is essential to the other. A young person must come to know the acceptance and warmth of mutuality before he can be a significant person to others. Without mutuality his mission activity can be self-serving and motivated out of a need to buttress his self-importance.

Likewise, a sense of mission is essential to an experience of mutuality. The danger of mutuality alone is that people can develop an in-group mentality that never looks beyond family concerns. A preoccupation with in-group feelings can become, in its extreme form, "navel-gazing."

I see our ministry as basically one of encouraging mutuality and then participating with youth in bringing about what we together hope for. Our task is to awaken the sense of the possible and then become involved in the mission which the hopes create. For the Christian the elements of hope are found in the message he bears. Because of Jesus Christ, he believes there is hope for everyone, regardless of his situation. He is convinced that there is good news for every person. For no one can it be said that everything is hopeless. This conviction I believe will penetrate all that a youth worker does and says. In short, he will incarnate God's resurrection "yes" to man. He will convey the fact that another person's life can be significant because every promise of God speaks of possibilities, possibilities that are summed up in the person of Jesus Christ.

Our calling is to discover a new creation and a new generation. This is in the realm of God's possibilities.

Bibliography

Blood, Robert, and Wolfe, Donald. *Husbands and Wives: The Dynamics of Married Living.* New York: Free Press, 1960.

Bronfenbrenner, Urie, and Condry, John C., Jr. *Two Worlds of Childhood: U.S. and U.S.S.R.* New York: Russell Sage Foundation, 1970.

Carkhuff, R., and Truax, C. "Training in Counseling and Psychotherapy: An Evaluation of an Integrated Didactic and Experiential Approach." *Journal of Counseling Psychology* (1965) 29, 333-336.

Douglas, J. "Youth in Turmoil: America's Changing Youth Cultures and Student Protest Movements." *Crime and Delinquency Issues: a Monograph Series* (1970) No. NIH-69-1121, Center for Studies of Crime and Delinquency, National Institute of Mental Health, Washington, D.C.

Douvan, E., and Adelson, J. B. *The Adolescent Experience.* New York: John Wiley, 1966.

Erb, F. *The Development of the Young People's Movement.* Chicago: University of Chicago Press, 1917.

Eysenck, H. "Primary Social Attitudes: I. The Organization and Measurement of Social Attitudes." *International Journal of Opinion and Attitude Research* (1947) I, 49-84.

Feuer, L. S. *Conflict of Generations.* New York: Basic Books, 1969.

Gordon, T. *Parent Effectiveness Training: The "No-lose" Way for Raising Responsible Children.* New York: Wyden, 1970.

Heath, D. H. *Growing Up in College: Liberal Education and Maturity.* San Francisco: Jossey-Bass, 1968.

Heath, D. *Humanizing Schools: New Directions, New Decisions.* New York: Hayden, 1971.

Hill, Reuben. *Family Development in Three Generations.* Cambridge, Mass. and London: Schenkman, 1970.

Johnston, Jerome, and Bachman, Jerald G. *Young Men Look at Military Service: Preliminary Report.* Ann Arbor: Survey Research Institute, Institute for Social Research, The University of Michigan, 1971.

Keniston, Kenneth. *Young Radicals: Notes on Committed Youth.* New York: Harcourt, Brace and World, 1968.

Lewis, L. "The Value of College to Different Subcultures." In *Contemporary Adolescence: Readings,* ed. H. D. Thornburg. Belmont, California: Brooks/Cole, 1971.

Life (May 16, 1969). "What People Think About Their High Schools: A Survey by Louis Harris."

Lipset, Seymour, and Schaftlander, Gerald M. *They'd Rather Be Left.* Boston: Little, Brown, 1971.

Little, Sara. *Youth, World, and Church.* Richmond, Virginia: John Knox, 1968.

Mead, Margaret. *Culture and Commitment: A Study of the Generation Gap.* Garden City, New York: Natural History Press/ Doubleday, 1970.

Moynihan, D. "Nirvana Now." *The American Scholar* (Autumn, 1967) 539-548, 36.

Musgrove, Frank. *Youth and the Social Order.* London: Routledge and Kegan Paul. New York: Humanities Press, 1965.

National Directory of Hotlines, Switchboard, and Related Services (1972). Minneapolis: The Exchange, 331 Cedar Avenue South.

Reich, Charles. *The Greening of America.* New York: Random House, 1970.

Resources for Youth (1971). New York: National Commission on Resources for Youth, 36 West 44th Street, New York, 10036.

Roszak, Theodore. *The Making of a Counter Culture: Reflections on the Technocratic Society and Its Youthful Opposition.* Garden City, New York: Doubleday, 1969.

Schofield, William. *Psychotherapy: The Purchase of Friendship.* Englewood Cliffs, N.J.: Prentice-Hall, 1964.

Stewart, Charles W. *Adolescent Religion: A Developmental Study of the Religion of Youth.* Nashville: Abingdon Press, 1967.

Strommen, Merton P., ed. *Research in Religious Development: A Comprehensive Handbook.* New York: Hawthorn, 1971.

Strommen, Merton P., Brekke, Milo L., Underwager, Ralph C., and Johnson, Arthur L. *A Study of Generations.* Minneapolis: Augsburg Publishing, 1972.

Thornburg, Hershel D., ed. *Contemporary Adolescence: Readings.* Belmont, California: Brooks-Cole, 1971.

Weiner, Irving B. *Psychological Disturbance in Adolescence.* New York: Wiley-Interscience, 1967.

Yankelovich, Daniel. *The Changing Values on Campus: Political and Personal Attitudes of Today's College Students.* New York: Washington Square Press, 1972.